Live Wealthy Retire Happy

Embracing Human Experiences to Live a Life of Abundance

CORA Z. CARDENAS

First published by Ultimate World Publishing 2026
Copyright © 2026 Cora Cardenas

ISBN

Paperback: 978-1-923583-62-7
Ebook: 978-1-923583-63-4

Cover design: Ultimate World Publishing
Layout and typesetting: Ultimate World Publishing
Editor: Carmela Julian Valencia

Ultimate World Publishing
Diamond Creek,
Victoria Australia 3089
www.writeabook.com.au

Dedication

This book is dedicated to my readers and my clients. You gave me the courage to share my story.

This is also dedicated to my mother, Concepcion Uranza Zamora, whose wisdom was my compass, her sacrifices my foundation. May her unwavering strength, generosity and love teach us all the meaning of true wealth.

Mum lived by the quiet command: 'Do not be a burden. Always add value.' Her voice echoes on every page, guiding me still. Rest in eternal paradise, my dear mother.

Acknowledgements

To my beloved husband, Eric, thank you for giving me the space to tick this off my bucket list, another one of my dreams come true; for being my constant and steadfast companion through every season – your support, encouragement and our shared dreams have been the bedrock of this journey. Your love continues to be my greatest wealth.

To my siblings, you are my first circle of wisdom and laughter. From childhood stories to grown-up prayers, our values, shared memories of hardship, resilience, days of fun and bonding, unrelenting support, inspiring achievements and love constantly remind me that family is a lifelong treasure.

To my children, you are my legacy and my joy. Watching you grow has been my richest reward. May this book be a guidepost for you to live fully, give generously and retire happy and fulfilled. To Craig, especially, you are my inspiration for my authoring journey. You have given me the strength and resolve to follow your unpaved path.

To everyone who is part of this book, thank you for your presence in my life. Your names have been changed to protect your privacy, but you will recognise yourselves and your contribution to my human puzzle.

To my team – my editor, Carmela Valencia; my mentors, Vivienne Mason, Julie Fisher, Stuart Denman; Lendy Macario, Nikola Boskovski, Velin Saramov; my publisher, Natasa Denman – you have all been amazing. I wouldn't have done this without your help and support. Thank you.

This book is not just mine. It is ours – woven from love, inspiration and shared hope. Thank you for being part of the story, my human experience.

Disclaimer

This book is intended for inspirational and educational purposes only. It reflects personal experiences, values and perspectives on wealth, retirement and life fulfilment. It is not intended to provide financial, investment, legal or professional advice.

Readers are encouraged to consult qualified professionals before making any financial or investment decisions. The author and publisher disclaim any liability for actions taken based on the content of this book.

Real names of people have been changed in this book, except in cases where permission was obtained to use real names.

Contents

Introduction

I am sitting in my office, waiting for my client to arrive. I am reading the background information why the client wants to see me.

I pause. 'I know what to do.'

Client case:

Female, 35 years old, with one dependent child, has part-time work. Her husband is sick and can't work, and they have no insurance. They cannot pay their electricity bill. They are late with their rent and are at risk of eviction. They have barely enough money to shop for food and groceries this week. Her daughter is attending a private school. They are also late with school fees, and she can't join the school excursion. She's stressed and doesn't know what to do or who to turn to. They have no family in Sydney.

Before the appointment, I am brought back to memory lane. My poor mum was in the same situation many years ago, but her circumstances were far worse than this client's. Mum had six dependent children and no income. She was a stay-at-home mum relying on Dad's income. My dad didn't have permanent work, but we studied in private schools. We faced several evictions. We can't pay our electricity bills. We barely had food on our table. A few times, our electricity supply has been disconnected. There was no form of community support where we came from, and my mum had to deal with this all by herself.

My poor mum. Nobody listened to her story. But today I'm listening to my client as if I'm listening to my mum's story.

Every day, it is as if I'm listening to my own stories of hardship.

I assure my client that this service is private and confidential. It is a free community service run by volunteers with adequate qualification and a license to practice. I explain to her the process of the appointment, we sign the paperwork and proceed with the intake process. I continue with the assessment, respectfully asking questions about how she came to this point and what the main thing is that she wants to get out of this session. I present information and options to guide her throughout the process, and we work on an action plan together.

As the client talks to me, she realises her own issues, owns up to it and comes up with her own solutions. She accepts her situation. She wants to make changes and move forward.

I provide support and referrals. She leaves, relieved and happy with a referral letter to the Emergency Relief department for an electricity voucher, a couple of bags containing basic food and groceries, a letter to her real estate agent, and a sheet of paper that says 'Action Plan'. She states that she feels so much better than when she first came in, as if the weight of the world has been lifted from her shoulders.

She thanks me for such relief, that someone listened to her.

Every day, I listen to client stories. Every day, it seems like I know what to do and how to help them. Every day comes so naturally for me. Like fish in the water, I can just swim and navigate through the vast ocean of life issues; not that I'm a genius in life, but because I've been through so many human experiences, I can totally relate.

Every day, I hear my late mum saying, 'What did you learn from that experience?' I can feel her tough love and see the 'scary mum' look on her face, imprinted in my noggin. Every day, I can see my late dad giving me a quiet smile of approval, 'Good job'. Every day reminds me of my late father-in-law always saying, 'I regret.'

Every day, I am grateful and happy. This is my retirement years.

I work two days a week at the local community centre as a financial counsellor. I specialise in counselling clients whose issues stem from money. Money touches every aspect of human life. When one does not have money or does not know how to manage money, it can cause stress, illness and, worse, death. It can affect physical and mental health, relationships, study, work and family life.

I help my clients obtain a long-term, sustainable solution for their current issues. I work with clients who are willing to own and be responsible for their issues. They need to be ready for change and to take action.

I worked for 25 years in corporate finance. I was then dealing with a $250 million budget for my department – very complex, extremely complex. But in the last 15 years, after a career change to counselling, I am now dealing with $250 budget for my clients. Such an enormous shift, and even more complexities to deal with.

Corporate work was good, but it was not for me. The long hours of number crunching, the never-ending month-end, quarter-end and year-end deadlines were so stressful. The office politics. The repetitive ongoing routine of recording, monitoring, analysing, reconciling data and ensuring the integrity of financial outcomes. The constantly changing KPI goal posts. The stress of having to deal with managers and colleagues with difficult behaviour. The ever-changing upgrade of IT systems, change-over projects and go-live dates.

I used to feel so drained and empty after each workday. It was such a thankless job. I kept going for 25 years until I was forced out through a redundancy. I spent years of undergraduate degree and more years of postgraduate degree to get this job. I spent years of experience honing my skills. I thought this was the job for me. This was what my mum wanted for me. This made her proud. I wanted to make her proud because of all her pains and sacrifices. It was my life mission to make her happy.

Twenty-five years of corporate finance was a human experience. I developed great friendships over time. It developed my skills, paid our bills and provided us well enough. It helped build our home. It sharpened my financial literacy skills. It broadened my knowledge. The corporate jungle toughened me up. Yet, it was not what nourished my soul.

After being forced out of corporate finance, it gave me the opportunity to pursue my desire for what would enrich my spirit and nurture my inner self.

Counselling is where I belong. I was always drawn towards human behaviour. I wanted to deal with people, and not numbers. I wanted to listen to stories of life. I wanted to understand people's behaviour. Yet, the 25 years of corporate finance made me proficient in finance. I didn't want to throw away something I became an expert in — all my 25 years of finance education, skills, experience and hard work. I didn't know how to shift from finance to something else that deals with human behaviour. I was at a crossroads. It was all too confusing.

One day, by chance, by coincidence, by God's grace, I saw an ad in the local paper needing financial counsellors. I didn't even know there was such a thing.

Like the heavens opening a gate of opportunity for me, I navigated this new path. A perfect combination of counselling and my finance skills and experiences.

I am now over 15 years into listening to my clients' stories — thousands of stories, same human life with different iterations of hardship and choices and circumstances.

Every night after my workdays at the community centre, I come home so satisfied and fulfilled. I have helped yet another soul, I say to myself. That's my pay forward.

My sister, who has a collection of many things, once asked me, 'What do you collect?' She knows I love to travel. 'Probably artwork from Europe, rugs from Turkey, glass from Venice, blue tiles from Portugal, llama products from Peru, *Made in China* key chains, fridge magnets, pins, baseball caps, shirts, souvenir items from different cities?'

I could not answer her question then. I don't like knick-knacks that can add to my already cluttered space. But now I can sincerely answer. I say to myself, 'Thank you, cards. Thank you, emails. Thank you, flowers. Thank you, drawings of little children. Thank you, hugs of relief.' That's what I collect – gratitude.

I realised that not everyone is capable of saying thank you and being grateful. Not everyone is capable of acknowledging the support that they receive. That does not diminish the value that I have lovingly and sincerely shared to those who have no capacity to see it. I know in my heart that for every one precious thank you, there are a few more unspoken gratitude whose life I have touched and positively changed.

My *thank you* collection is a testament that I am doing the job that heaven assigned for me. I begin with gratitude, and so I end with gratitude. Because gratitude unlocks abundance in life.

Many years ago, in 1991, I migrated to Australia from the Philippines with my husband, Eric, and our two small children. We left everything behind. We started from almost nothing but eight balikbayan boxes of personal items. We were so young, sad, lonely, anxious, scared and, at the same time, excited, brave enough, ready and determined to make new beginnings and looking forward to a bright future in a new country.

Today, here we are – Eric, all his three brothers and their wives and children, his sister and her husband, his mum and dad, my sister and her husband and their two children. We are healthy, surrounded by a loving extended family and circle of supportive and caring friends. We have enough money to spend. We have the freedom of time and movement.

We've been blessed.

My mum and dad have instilled the principle of reciprocity in all six of us, their children. When we receive, we have to give back more than what we received. Even in my difficult childhood days, my parents didn't have much, but they still gave a lot of the little that they had.

Gratitude is definitely my attitude.

Australia has provided the platform for us to have a life of abundance. We have taken that opportunity, not without challenge nor a faint heart. We embraced every human experience with a positive response and with the mindset of growth, giving back and paying forward.

Today, it's time to tell my stories.

1

Random life stories and puzzle pieces

We are not human beings having a spiritual experience.
We are spiritual beings having a human experience.
– Wayne Dyer

I always believe that we are all sent from heaven, with millions of pieces of our own jigsaw puzzle. Each of us has our own puzzle that we put together through life. Each piece is different and equally valuable. Each piece is a gold nugget.

Each piece of our puzzle is our own human experience as part of a bigger whole. By itself, a piece on its own does not make sense. But as we put the pieces together and fit them perfectly, slowly, an image unfolds. In this divine unfolding, we begin to understand what we didn't see before. When a full puzzle is completed, our big picture is revealed.

Earthquake

'Marylou! Marylou! Marylou!' my 35-year-old mum calls out my 11-year-old sister's name in panic at around 4 am. Still half asleep on the third floor of our almost run-down apartment are my 9-year-old sister, 7-year-old brother and me. The barking of the dogs and the sound of bottles breaking, things crashing down and walls collapsing awaken us. It's still very dark, and everything is rocking side to side. Stuff around the house are falling and being thrown everywhere.

My dad was absent. He was an overseas contract worker in Vietnam.

Today, in August 1968, Manila is struck by one of the strongest recorded earthquakes at 7.3 magnitude. It's called the Ruby Tower Earthquake because the Ruby Tower in Manila, 7 kilometres from where we live, collapsed, killing at least 250 residents.

Tomorrow, I will be turning 6. My birthday is a non-event regardless. We rarely celebrated birthdays because it was just another day. We're just happy we survived this catastrophe.

Haemorrhagic fever

In 1965, I was playing with my cousins at home in Malate, Manila. It was a very happy day with my aunts and cousins. The next thing I knew, I was in the hospital, and my nose was bleeding profusely. I had so many red spots all over my body. My body temperature was 40°C. I vaguely recall that I was placed inside a rectangular medical tent, a device to cool and regulate my body temperature.

Mum said I suffered from H fever, also known as dengue fever or viral haemorrhagic fever (VHF). According to Mum, there was an epidemic of VHF at that time and a lot of children died. She was very scared that I'd suffer the same fate and was happy that I survived.

'Anything from here on is a bonus for you,' she said.

At 3 years old, I am living my second lease in life. Everything is a bonus.

A near car crash

It's an ordinary day in 1964. Mum was inside the house doing the laundry and house chores as a stay-at-home mum. *Bang!* The sound of a car suddenly hitting its brakes could be heard in front of our house.

The driver yells out in anger, frustration and shock. 'Hey, *Misis*! Can you look after your child properly.'

Mum runs out as quickly as she can to pick me up. I was in my cloth diapers crossing the street, shocked and oblivious to what I had done wrong. My poor mum – so distressed from an already busy day 'in her office', and then this. Someone left the gates open, and I must have done a walkabout out of curiosity.

This was my first near death experience at 18 months old.

Christmas in Saigon

Dad worked in Air America. He was assigned in Saigon, Vietnam in the late 1960s. We missed him so much, and he missed us too. He was not allowed to go home for Christmas in 1968, so he arranged for his family to visit him in Saigon.

Everyone in our family took us to the airport in a convoy of jeeps and cars. I think it was all my aunts, uncles, some cousins and grandma, mostly travelling from the province, wishing us bon voyage and sending us off to the airport for our two-week holiday in Saigon.

I remember walking across the tarmac in our best Sunday clothes. There was an official photographer at the bottom of the stairs to the aircraft, and we posed for posterity. I can imagine my beautiful mum in her beautiful outfit as Jackie Kennedy.

It was an amazing first airplane ride on Pan Am 747. We received freebies of colouring books, crayons, puzzles and some soft toys. The lavatory was filled with luxury perfumes and scented little soaps.

'Hey, if you go to the bathroom, you will find plenty of stuff! Look, I got some,' my brother whispered in my ear.

It was one of the most amazing feelings – going away on a holiday with Mum and my siblings and getting all these free stuff.

But, Saigon in 1968? Really? What were they thinking? It was the height of the Vietnam War! But it was fun for us. We spent time with Dad, and we were a family at Christmastide. Mum and Dad and some of his friends were with us all the time. We stayed in Uncle Pete's house.

My brother and I thought it was all games. After all, the games we played with were those little green soldier dolls, machine guns, a helicopter drone, Tommy toy guns, small aircraft carriers and lots of battlefield toys. I was 6, and he just turned 8. In all innocence and naivety, we felt no danger at all as we embarked on this trip.

In reality, there were soldiers with machine guns; barbed wires around the city; plumes of smoke; the smell of burning metals;

the sound of bombs, gun shots and sirens; the sound of helicopter landings; women and children running and scampering around; and armoured personnel vehicles roaming all over the city. At night, we were asked to keep quiet. We could hear the heavy footsteps of soldiers walking through the roof and around the house.

One night, I played a trick on everyone and locked the outside bathroom door and crawled under the gap, leaving the door locked. Upon waking up in the morning, Uncle Pete wanted to use the toilet and found it locked. He panicked and woke up everyone, saying that a Viet Cong is hiding in the bathroom, so beware.

Everyone was so anxious the whole time, thinking we were invaded by the enemies; anytime, we could all be captured. We were on the American side – my dad was working with Air America. Everyone started to pray for safety. My dad was ready to evacuate all of us to another city. I was too scared to tell the truth that it was me. I thought it was fun. I didn't realise the gravity of my practical joke.

I told Dad I can crawl under the door and unlock it. I was tiny enough to do that. I said, if there was a Viet Cong inside the cubicle, wouldn't we be able to see his legs between the gap?

Smart-ass me. Scared as they were, I was able to convince them that it was safe for me to do it. So, I did it. *After all, I just had to undo what I did the night before.* What a fake little hero, was I!

We could not get out of Saigon as planned, as the bombings got worse. We went to Da Nang Air Base via a Black Hawk helicopter, and from there we flew back to Manila in time for school. *Phew!* We survived.

At 6, I had my first wartime adventure.

Floods

We lived in Arellano Avenue for most of my childhood. It is a typical street of Manila. Some parts are beautiful with high-gated compounds and lovely gardens, and some parts of the avenue looked like a squatter's area. There is a creek that runs parallel to the avenue and a bridge north of the avenue. Near the foot of the bridge, some homeless people have built rooms out of cardboard boxes and discarded building materials, polluting the beautiful creek with their rubbish and human waste.

Arellano Avenue is a street between Vito Cruz and Zobel Roxas, both of which are built on the high side of the city. Arellano Avenue looks like a valley between these two high streets. Every year during typhoon season, due to heavy rains and clogged sewerage, the creek would overflow. The flood waters from Vito Cruz and Zobel Roxas would meet and gather exactly where we live. Every year, we experience flooding in our small apartment. Flood water would enter our apartment, sometimes, waist deep. This would happen at least once every single year. Sometimes, it would occur twice to four times a year.

It was something we would just deal with, like it's just normal. We would be ready to move our furniture to the upper floor. We had a platform permanently built for our piano. We would stack our furniture and appliances on top of the dining table and Dad's office table. If the flood water wasn't too high, we would use our dining chairs and connect them to form a bridge to walk around the house without our feet getting wet.

We had animals and pets (chicken, pigs, dogs, cats) that would be moved up to the bedrooms upstairs. During days when floodwater stalled inside the house, Mum would cook at the balcony upstairs.

She would organise meals like we were at camp, cooking with charcoal with a portable, improvised stove. Everyone and everything – people, animals, furniture, personal belongings, food, cooking utensils, school stuff, clutter – would be upstairs, cramped into our two-bedroom apartment.

When the rain would stop and the floodwaters would begin to recede, my mum and dad would be on watch duty 24 hours, monitoring the movement of the flood to ensure they cleaned up downstairs at exactly the same time the water receded. This helps to wash the debris in the flow with the floodwater. If they miss out on this exact time, there will be a lot of mud and debris left inside every corner of the house, everywhere. The stench of the floodwater would stay for days and weeks on end.

The thing is, there's so much floodwater everywhere. Yet, there's so little clean water we can use to mop up the debris. They had to use the same floodwater to clean the dirt that has caused it.

After each flood, I'd witness how exhausted my parents would be, especially Mum. Moving furniture, organising the kids, the pets, the cooking arrangements, the cleanup, and seeing all the damage caused – it was traumatising to watch. Yet, this happened every single year. Year after year after year.

For many years, Mum was probably numbed by all this trauma. She just kept on going. In fact, she probably developed a system to manage it. She had no choice. This was the only accommodation we could afford. We had to put up with it.

I lived in Arellano Avenue until the end of 1984, when I got married. When I left, I promised myself that in the future, when I have my own family, I will never allow my children to experience such trauma.

Fire

One day in 1980, Mum went to the market, her usual routine after taking my little sisters to school. I was in my first year of university, and I had left for my class. My brother had also left for his class. By this time, both my elder sisters have left home, now living and working in the USA. It was just my mum with us, her four children. Dad wasn't there.

I got home after class, around 4 pm, and there was chaos and commotion in our street. There were two fire trucks and so many people gathered together – some watching, some looting, some trying to save things, some helping, some crying, some just as confused as everyone else.

As I walked towards home, I realised that it was our whole apartment compound that had been gutted. I felt numb. There was so much water everywhere from all the firefighting. The smell of burnt wood and other materials was suffocating. There was fire, but it seemed that it was under control now.

Where's my mum? I hurriedly walked towards the gate to our compound and saw all the burnt apartments – Zero, A, B, C, D. There were only five apartments. We occupied apartment C.

My mum was sitting inside our house, in shock and crying.

'I just went to the market. It was just a quick trip,' she said. 'When I came close to home, our neighbours asked me to stop and not go home. People recognised me as Puti's mum.' My brother, Bert, was quite popular in our neighbourhood. He was very fair, and they called him *Puti* (meaning *white*) because he made friends with all the dark-skinned and sun-tanned boys at the outdoor basketball court.

'They said they tried to save as much as they could from our burning house. The neighbours were so good. They were guarding our little possessions from the looters. I don't know what to do.'

Bert's friends forced open our front door and took out whatever furniture they could, placed them in a nearby safe spot and guarded them from looters. They went in and out of our house several times, doing this as many times as possible to save as many belongings as they could salvage. But it felt like we lost everything. It was devastating to lose almost everything to fire. Not that we had plenty to lose, but it seemed that we lost all the little that we had, despite the neighbour's heroic efforts.

There is a Filipino saying: *Manakawan ka na ng sampung beses. Wag ka lang masunugan.* (It is better to experience theft 10 times than experience fire once.)

This was our one time.

But Mum saw this as a true blessing. Everything inside our apartment was wet and soggy from the water bombing. Everything smelled burnt. The fire started from Apartment Zero, then spread through Apartment D. They were all gutted and charred, but the fire seemed to skip Apartment C, and we were spared. It was incredible how it happened. It was a miracle!

Mum had a Christ the King altar at the entrance of our apartment. We used to pray the rosary every day at 6 pm in front of this altar. Mum believed that it was our Christ the King statue that protected our home and saved us.

My mum refused to leave our apartment in a smouldering mess. For weeks, and maybe months, we reeked of the stench of burnt wood and the stinky smell of smoke and musty water. Our hair, skin, clothes and shoes smelled burnt. It was awful.

Home and content insurance was unheard of then. Well, even if it were a 'thing' then, we wouldn't have been able to afford it, anyway. I don't know how we moved on from there.

It is what it is. We were gutted by fire, but we survived.

Rainbow

When my dad passed away, I felt that there was so much I wanted to tell him that I didn't have the opportunity to say when he was alive. After a few days of him passing, Eric woke me up from my sleep as I gasped for air like I was choking.

I dreamt that Dad called me. He said I could talk to him if I wanted to. I could say anything, and he would not be upset. So, I started talking, and he led me to a beautiful place. We kept walking over a meadow of flowers, green scenery and a big, quiet lake. He walked through the lake so easily, and I realised I could not go through the lake the way he was walking on it. I tried to walk around the lake, but it was too far. I tried to cross, but I sank and could not get through.

I was awoken when, in my dream, I was drowning.

In reality, I stopped breathing. That night, I didn't use my CPAP machine (a breathing device to help with my collapsing airways), and I was gasping for breath.

In our language, there is a word called *bangungot* to describe death by nightmare, or a sudden unexplained nocturnal death when healthy people die in their sleep. Sometimes, it may be due to oxygen deprivation as one endlessly gasp for air.

'Dad wanted to take you with him. Next time, don't go with him. You're not ready to die yet. If you want to speak to him again in your dreams, just speak to him, but don't go with him,' Marylou said after I told her my experience. As a nurse, she always has practical medical evidence based information to explain human body responses, so I was surprised to hear what she had to say after that nightmare story. I would have expected her to say something like, 'You forgot to wear your CPAP machine, that's why you were gasping for air.' But since that time, I kept her words in my head.

One night, I had another dream. Dad and I were inside a taxi, having a conversation. We were travelling through a city, though I could not recognise where. There were people walking, talking, working and going through their normal day. It was a bit cloudy. The dad I was with was my dad in his 20s. He looked very young, vibrant and full of life. He looked like his photos when he worked in Wake Island – his clothes, his haircut, his skin, his youthful smile. Although I could not recall what we were talking about, it felt good that I was with him, even in my dream.

'Dad, how are you?' I asked him.

He looked at me in quiet approval. 'Oh, don't ask me how I am,' he said. 'I want to know how you are. I'll tell you how I am. Just look to your left, I am there.'

Everything happened quickly. The taxi driver went past the streets, and we were taken to another place of quiet, green space, blue space, white space, then a beautiful rainbow appeared. It was like magic. I turned to Dad in overwhelm and wanted to hug him and thank him, but he was no longer in the taxi.

I woke up wondering if this was a dream or a message from Dad, a message from heaven. I don't know, but it was a very good feeling. A feeling beyond words I cannot describe. It was like I spoke to Dad about everything I wanted to tell him without saying a word, and everything was ok. It was a soothing feeling, knowing that Dad is in a good place, like the rainbow. It was such a magical moment.

From then on, I relied on the magic of rainbows. Every rainbow I see is a reminder that Dad is there, and I can talk to him without saying a word, and everything will be ok.

Lesson 1: Earthquakes, floods, fires, accidents, and illnesses are all part of a human experience. So are rainbows.

2

Ordinary me

Becoming wealthy is not a matter of how much you earn,
who your parents are, or what you do. It's a matter of
managing your money properly.
– Noel Whittaker, Australian Finance writer

I am ordinary. I come from an ordinary family. I have no special talent in anything – not in maths, science, arts, singing, music, dancing, sports, academics or public speaking. I grew up in ordinary environments and ordinary circumstances. I have ordinary dreams and life goals.

I was raised to be a good, simple person living an ordinary life. Go to church. Believe in God. Listen to parents and elders. Establish good relationships. Be respectful. Eat healthy. Study hard. Finish a university degree. Be a good human being. Find decent work. Save for a rainy day. Contribute to society. Find a husband. Be a good wife. Have kids. Raise my children well. Buy a house. Pay it off. Save money for my retirement. Live life well.

We've had some interesting stories to tell with earthquakes, war, floods, fires, illnesses, peaceful revolutions and a bit more. Otherwise, there's nothing much exceptional.

Live life **well**. That's what Mum tells me.

Being a millionaire was not part of this agenda. For me and my family, being a millionaire was only possible if we won a lottery ticket. My dad used to regularly buy lottery tickets, wishing and believing he'd end up being a wealthy one. But, of course, he never won.

Client case:

Female, 42 years old. Husband is incarcerated. Client needs help with debt management, mainly her mortgage arrears and business debts. She is suffering from mental health issues. Client works fulltime. They won the lotto.

Today's case is not about having no money but my client winning the lottery. They won $10 million. I did the usual financial assessment for my client and listened to her story.

Her husband is in jail. She is highly stressed because she has already lost her investment property, and now she is at risk of losing her house.

It baffles me that she won $10 million in the lottery, and yet she's here with all these issues.

She wishes they had never won the lotto. They had it all good before the lotto win, but now everything is ruined. Before winning the lotto, they were ahead on their home mortgage. They even had an investment property, which was also doing well. She and her husband had fulltime employment, and they were living ordinary lives. They were happy.

When they won the lotto, her husband was lured into buying businesses that promised passive income so one day they would not have to work their nine-to-five jobs. With all the excitement of their windfall income, her husband, without doing adequate research and due diligence, got involved and purchased a telecom shop. He didn't even know anything about running it, trusting that his friend would manage it well.

The business did well during the first few months, experiencing exponential growth. His friend encouraged them to invest more, which they did. On top of the lotto winning, they took loans out of their equity in their investment property to expand the businesses. They even invited her husband's sister to invest money in their growing businesses, which she did. The sister also took out loans to invest.

Unbeknownst to them, the businesses they bought were shopfronts linked to drugs, underworld crime and money laundering. The police were already keeping an eye on those managing the businesses they now own, and they planned their raid on a day that the manager friend was away on holiday. While her husband and his sister were cluelessly taking care of the day-to-day operations, the police raided their house, looking for the shop manager and the owner. Apparently, some inventory were stocked in their house. They did not know that these were illegal drugs, and the police found them.

My client could not believe what happened when she received a phone call from the police that her husband was in custody. She was totally shocked. The manager friend had escaped with most of their money and could no longer be found. The businesses were sequestered. Their investment property was now gone. The $10 million lotto winning vanished in thin air. The sister-in-law lost her investment, declared bankruptcy and disowned them. The family was ruined.

I was almost speechless and quite fascinated with this unusual client case. I discussed options with the client on how she wants to proceed, and I could help with a short-term solution to advocate for a moratorium to ensure she is not left homeless in the next three months. For the long term, she needs to make a decision on what her intentions would be, given the results of the financial assessment.

The client was happy that someone listened to her story with compassion – no judgment, no shame, no blame, just active listening. She left with a bag of food and groceries, a referral letter to the psychologist, an Options Sheet for her husband to help them decide the next steps and an Action Plan to contact her home loan provider for a moratorium.

The dream of being a millionaire

It was exceptional to be a millionaire five to six decades ago. But today, it has just become the reach of the ordinary. According to the 2025 UBS Global Wealth Report, one in every ten Australian adults is a millionaire. There are approximately 1.9 million US-dollar millionaires in Australia. In Australian dollar terms, there are 2.8 million millionaires in Australia. In the world, there are approximately 59.4 million US-dollar millionaires. That's overwhelming for me!

With the average house prices in Australia recently passing the million-dollar mark, most homeowners are now millionaires, like ordinary me. I'm just one of those happy statistics.

No, I didn't win $10 million. I am not my client. I am not my dad. I don't rely on chance winnings. I rely on good money management and investing. Each time I receive my dividends, I feel like winning the lottery.

Winning the lottery does not necessarily make one wealthy. Like in anything in life, it is something you have to be ready for. You have to be prepared to manage your newfound fortune. Money management is a skill that needs to be mastered. Otherwise, if you are not ready for a sudden windfall income, it can ruin your life. There are so many horror stories of people winning the lottery and ending up in worse situations than where they originally started from.

Some tips to ponder on regarding this case:

- Invest in something that you understand. Do your own research when parting with your money.
- If you seriously think that winning the lottery is your ticket to financial freedom and regularly spend your money on this, know your odds in winning the lottery (Powerball: one in 134,490,400; Lotto: one in 38,320,568). In the event that you are the lucky winner, be confident that you know how to manage your winnings. Make sure you have a plan.
- Learn from the experiences of others – their mistakes and failures. Be inspired by other people's quiet success.
- Do not rely on get-rich-quick schemes. Be patient and get wealthy slowly through legitimate investments.
- Be aware of your relationship with money and your money behaviour. Understand the meaning of money.

Lesson No 2: Understand basic financial literacy.
Use it to your advantage.

3

Hardships

Hardships, poverty and want are the best incentives,
and the best foundation, for the success of man.
– Bradford Merrill

Memories of high-end poverty

I thought I was ordinary, but I overrated myself. We grew up poor in the city of Manila. It was strange that I thought poor since, together with my sisters, we attended private girls' schools throughout elementary and high school. Mum and Dad always believed that private education was important to build a good foundation for learning. My grandmother's sister was a school teacher at St Paul College of Manila (now St Paul University of Manila), and she was adamant that my dad should send us to this school, which was one of the most exclusive and expensive private girls' schools then.

This school was attended by the country's elite, such as daughters of high-ranking politicians, celebrities, industrialists and big business owners. Most of my classmates were children of professionals – doctors, lawyers, accountants, bankers, architects, engineers, government officials, high-ranking military men, showbiz celebrities, famous musicians and athletes. Then there's me and my sisters. My dad was a humble employee of a Chinese businessman. Before then, he worked as an admin officer in Air America. He was based in Wake Island, a coral atoll in the western Pacific Ocean. For a time, Dad was also based in Saigon, Vietnam as an overseas contract worker. He thought he had saved enough money and could establish a business in Manila with his friend. They ventured into a car dealership with Avante Corporation, which failed and bankrupted him. A lawyer friend, a congressman in the fourth district of our province, helped Dad gain employment with his Chinese client, and Dad became the right-hand man of Mr Tan.

I remember years of hardship, not only in finance but in the absence of a father. We were six children, five girls and one boy.

Dad was pretty smart. During the earlier years, Mum and Dad had a foreign exchange business. Although we lived in a small apartment, on the third floor of an almost run-down apartment block, I saw plenty of cash – a drawer full of US dollars bundled in thousands. Mum would deliver door-to-door remittance of salary to overseas contract workers.

We lived in Remedios Street, one of the sought-after elite addresses in Malate, a leafy, high-end neighbourhood of the city, where the emerging wealthy and the old rich reside. This was very close to Manila Bay, a tourist area famous for its magnificent sunsets, and within walking distance to the historic Our Lady of Remedies Parish – Malate Church. This was close proximity to the elite and exclusive private girls' and boys' schools (Assumption Convent, St Paul College, De La Salle University, Ateneo de Manila), fashion designer precinct and bustling café culture. People in this area lived in high-walled mansions with well-maintained, manicured gardens. They have pretty dogs and cats, which are walked by uniformed maids.

Every Sunday, we attended mass at Malate Church, where the yard was like a carnival every week. I loved going to church, but my mum would drag me to walk home to stop me from turning green with envy. There were clowns, popcorn, balloons, ice cream. I can see the fashionable women of the community, the stylish cars, the children in their Sunday dresses and shoes. I would drool from seeing the children enjoy their pink cotton candies, caramel popcorn and ice cream, and admire their pretty Sunday clothes, some with matching bags and dainty handkerchiefs, hair accessories, lace socks and fashionable shoes. Meanwhile, I would wear a 7-year-old, twice-hand-me-down dress from my two older sisters and worn-out shoes that's outgrown both size and fashion.

My eyes would roll in envy from the luxury vehicles, with uniformed chauffeurs, they would hop in. Families gathered outside the churchyard after mass and proceeded to the popular Aristocrat restaurant, a couple of blocks from the church, for family lunch. I would dream of one day sitting at one of those tables overlooking the bay while enjoying lunch with my mum and dad and siblings. However, I could not recall a cotton candy or a caramel popcorn, let alone a Sunday family lunch after church . . . ever.

Orosa Street

Orosa Street is a street in the district of Malate fronting one of the gates of St Paul College. Across the gate is an exclusive apartment complex, where my wealthy schoolmates live. In front of the apartment complex are shops, restaurants and small boutiques. Along Orosa Street are beautiful homes to many Paulinians (what students attending St Paul were called). It was so convenient that they would just cross the street to school.

Behind the luxury apartment, across the school gate, is a service block of units where service providers seem to live. These are the maids, drivers, shop employees and general helpers. In 1966, we moved to the third floor of this block of units, as we could no longer afford the rent in Remedios Street.

The apartment unit looked like a train to me. There was a long corridor, a windowless bedroom immediately to the left, which was my mum and dad's bedroom, and a room across. Farther down were two more rooms to the right. Towards the left is a bit of space with a small study table. At the end of the long hall was our kitchen, dining area and bathroom cum laundry room. Ventilation and light were only on the right side of the apartment.

Mum leased out one room to some nursing students to help us pay for the rent. We occupied two rooms. I would sleep with my mum when Dad was overseas. Otherwise, all four of us children would share one room, which was also Mum's craft room, where she would make clothes and sew our school uniforms. They could barely afford to buy new school uniforms from this very expensive school.

There was a small ground in the compound, where children would play in the afternoon. We can only watch from our third-floor unit. Mum would not allow us to go outside, saying we don't belong here. Only the children living from the luxury apartments had the privilege of playing there.

It was no fun living in this third-floor, cramped train apartment. My two sisters, my brother and I would play by ourselves inside. Sometimes, our cousins would visit, and we would play. But the tenants from the second-floor apartment would bang the ceiling and yell, 'Stop the noise, stop the noise, stop the noise!' Mum would *ssshhh* us all the time to quiet us down in fear of being evicted, not knowing where to go.

One day, while Mum was away, my brother and I could not help but go out and play with the other children. One child was hurt, and we were accused of not only deliberately hurting the child but also stealing money. This was not true, of course.

One of the parents chased after us, screaming, 'I swear, I will pluck the eyeballs out of your eye sockets with my pocket knife! Get out here and confess! I remember your faces, you rascals!'

My brother and I ran as fast as we could until we got inside and hid in our unit. It was one of my heart-stopping moments as a child. At 4 years old, I was so traumatised that I never went out of our unit without my mum or dad.

School

In 1968, I started kindergarten at St Paul College. My sisters and I would just cross the street, and there was school. I loved going to school because it was fun. In later years, when Dad would miss out on paying school fees on time (because he did not have work), it was not fun at all. It was stressful. Some memories of my stressful days in school include not being able to complete a school project because Mum couldn't afford the materials for the project, not being able to join excursions, failing to participate in school activities, not getting school photos because we couldn't afford it, and not being able to take the final exams until all school fees have been paid.

Some days, when special sports uniforms were required and Mum didn't have the money to pay for them, my teachers would be harsh in scolding me and not allow me to join the sports programs. There were countless times when I didn't have the complete set of school stationery for the year. These were just basic school supplies like notebooks, writing pads, pens, pencils, scissors, crayons, and the like, yet I didn't have them. Some days, we'd go to school without breakfast because there was none available at home. Some days, we didn't have packed lunch.

On finals day, teachers have two announcements. The first announcement was for those who were exempted from the exams because they had already obtained above average to exceptional marks for the grading period. The second announcement was for students who were not allowed to take the final exams and were asked to leave the room because their school fees had not yet been fully paid. I would be asked to leave the room a few times. The embarrassment and humiliation as a child were immense.

Then, I found a strategy to avoid the embarrassment and humiliation: *If I had marks high enough to get an exemption from final exams, my name would be included in the first announcement, instead of the second embarrassing announcement.*

It motivated me to study so hard to ensure I was included in the exemption for high marks. This worked well for some subjects, but not all the time. Dad would be very proud of me, saying, 'Keep it up. You're doing well.'

The rah-rah cheer of Dad gave me some confidence, yet up to this day, I still wonder how I survived school.

Seeing my classmates having all provisions of recess and lunch, lunch money, a complete set of school books and supplies, materials for projects, uniforms for sports, access to excursions, and not having to worry about final exams made me so hungry for what I was missing and what I was so anxious about. I wanted what they have. Why couldn't I have them?

School Excursion at Las Brisas

I was in fourth grade, and we had an excursion to Las Brisas. I have a love-hate relationship with school excursions. While I enjoy the outdoors, I always felt left out. I didn't get to go to all the school excursions because we couldn't afford them most times. My classmates would have those extra-special packed lunches (delicious picnic food, chocolates, cakes, fruits, chips, drinks) and extra clothing and footwear and other accessories that I didn't have. I always felt that everyone had all of those things except me. I was the only one who didn't have any of this stuff. Whether it was true or not, that was how it felt like to me. Mum never packed anything special for me or for any of us; no chocolates or chips or juice. It made me feel really awkward.

This excursion was a visit to the Sisters of St Paul of Chartres House, which looked like a beautiful resort, where the nuns lived. There were picnic areas and a pool and playgrounds, a chapel and cloister, and a residence for the nuns. We were all encouraged to enjoy the day after our prayer activity with the nuns.

Everyone went swimming, and I envied them because they all seemed to know how to swim. They had beautiful swim costumes, goggles, life vests, nice warm towels, sunscreen and skin lotions. Mum couldn't even afford to send us to have swim lessons, let alone all these accessories. As they were enjoying the pool, one of my classmates asked me to join them. With enough prodding. I reluctantly went down the pool and joined them. How silly of me. I didn't even know how to swim. How could I play in the pool with them?

My classmate pushed me, as I was taking too much time going down.

No!

I slowly submerged in the water, as if in slow motion. Bubble, bubble, bubble as I gasp for air. I didn't realise that I was at the deep end of the pool. I couldn't swim. I was drowning. I couldn't breathe. I tried to call for help, but I couldn't. I waddled my way to the edge of the pool, struggling as I kept swallowing water. It felt like forever. Stupid me, I can't even float.

Finally, I got myself out of the pool without anyone's help. No one even noticed me, not even the girl who pushed me.

I lay, almost unconscious and shocked. I didn't tell anyone. I didn't want to cause a scene. I tried to cough out some of the water I swallowed.

Breathe in and breathe out. A few times, breathe in and breathe out.

I courageously picked myself up, got changed and pretended that nothing happened.

I went to the playground with the other girls and enjoyed myself. At lunchtime, I didn't have any special packed lunch. It turns out that some of my classmates had too much food, and they asked me to take some of their food because if they didn't finish it, they would be in trouble with their parents. I was happy to take them, I had nothing! It was wonderful. What a treat!

I got home that afternoon, still shaken from the pool incident, but happy with the shared lunch. I didn't tell my mum I had an incident in the pool. It doesn't matter, anyway. She'll just give me that scary mum look and say, 'What lesson did you learn from that?'

I swore to myself that one day, when I can afford it, I will take swimming lessons.

One day, I asked my mum and dad, 'Why am I different from my classmates?'

'You know, dear, your parents are poor. Their parents are wealthy. It doesn't mean that your classmates are wealthy and you are poor. We send you to this school for a firsthand experience to know the difference between poverty and wealth,' they replied. 'This is an opportunity for you to know what could be possible by experiencing what you don't have. For now, you are poor just like your parents, and your classmates are wealthy just like their parents. But you can change that.

'If you learn and take control of your life, one day you can be wealthy and you can provide all these that you want for yourself. Make right choices in life. Just remember these lessons from poverty. Do not be poor forever, because it is expensive to be poor. Also, remember that if you were born poor, it is not your fault. If you die poor, it is your responsibility.'

Lesson 3: Use the pains of poverty as a great motivator to get out of poverty. Embrace every piece of your puzzle.

4

Learnings from Mum –
It's expensive to be poor

Anyone who has ever struggled with poverty
knows how extremely expensive it is to be poor.
– James Baldwin

Being thrown into an environment of 'what could be possible', I learned early on that it is expensive to be poor. They were my mum's words. I didn't know that there was such a thing as the **Boots theory**.

The Boots theory is a term coined by English fantasy writer Sir Terry Pratchett in his novel, Men at Arms, illustrating the theory of socio-economic unfairness through the simple example of the boots. In the novel, Captain Sam Vines compares the rich spending $50 on a good-quality, comfortable pair of boots that lasts for years, keeping their feet dry. The poor would only be able to afford a cheap $10 pair of boots, just enough to last a season until the cardboard leaks. The next season, they would need to buy another $10 boots – and the next and the next. Over 10 seasons, they would have spent $100 on uncomfortable and leaky boots, while their rich counterpart would have enjoyed the $50 boots in comfort and dry feet, saving $50.

My mum encouraged us to keep learning, as it is our only ticket out of poverty to live enriched lives. Learn, learn, learn.

Both mum and dad ingrained in our beings that there is nothing they can give us except the gift of education. That was our inheritance from them. And what a fine gift to be educated under the tutelage of the Paulinian values. For years and up to now, it is with great pride and joy that I identify myself as a Paulinian, almost a privilege, reserved only for a few.

Despite my dad's financial hardships, we were able to continue and complete our elementary and high school education in such a prestigious private girls' school. Outside of school, once I am introduced as a Paulinian, it's as if a command of respect is immediately earned and a sense of confidence is attached, like I'm wearing a badge of honour just because I am a Paulinian. This was especially true in the Philippines, where school almost defines you as an individual. Just being a Paulinian seems to send a message that I am a person of good character and breeding, of class, good taste, high morale, finesse and refinement.

My educational experience in a private girls' school was exceptional. My learning experience involved all aspects of our being – spiritual, physical, emotional, social, moral and intellectual. Despite its high academic standards, it was not the academics that were the most important focus. It was the moulding of our innocent minds and the development of life skills and character as the future adults of the community. As a young child, the first question of teachers at kindergarten was, 'How can you make the world more beautiful and good?'

It was learning how to think, create and contribute. It was learning how to continuously adapt to our changing environments. It was learning the skills and confidence in navigating through life. It was the networking opportunities. It was being in an environment of children of nobility, groomed in class and decent taste. Just being around these children every day for many years had a great influence on me. I developed a strong desire to be one of them. Eventually, I became one of them.

My parents chose to send us to private schools with the Boots theory in mind, without even knowing it. Their principle was investing in our education. They would always argue that if private education was expensive, try free public education in a developing country. They believed that their children's private education was their ultimate sacrifice and investment.

My mum explained to me how economic unfairness exists, and a poor person pays more and has fewer opportunities for change. This was very true in the country where we grew up, where the power distance index is high, where the powerful rules and where the poor barely thrive.

She cited countless examples of the sad fact that it is expensive to be poor. Actually, she didn't have to cite these examples. We experienced them firsthand, and we lived them:

> **Food** – The poor are often limited in affording cheap food compared to their wealthy counterparts, who can spend more money on healthy and more nourishing food, which can oftentimes be more expensive. Healthy options are sometimes inaccessible and oftentimes unaffordable to poor people.
>
> By eating healthier food, the wealthy are healthier and sometimes even smarter. The wealthy have so many food

choices to nourish their bodies and brains. Brain growth, development and function are essential for a smart decision-making process that can lead to a wealthier life.

Health and recreation – Access to facilities like exercise, fitness centres, sports, music, arts, dance studios or wellness clinics is often unaffordable to poor people. These centres promote health, wellness and creativity. Poor people are often denied these experiences and may have to pay more further down their life by not developing healthy habits and creativity and not achieving their full potential.

Bulk purchasing – Wealthy people can purchase in bulk and get discounts and savings. In comparison, a poor individual with limited resources would buy in retail and small packets and pay more per unit of measure. That was us. Mum used to purchase small tubes of low-quality, cheap toothpaste. That was what she could afford. My aunt would purchase a packet of 12 large-size quality toothpaste tubes and would get two free, giving her small savings. These savings can be significant if added over the long term.

Home – Where we live is a factor in determining good opportunities, like good quality schools, good neighbourhood, facilities, environment and even role models. Wealthy people enjoy a better quality of life because of proximity to expansive spaces, expensive areas close to the beach, breathing fresh air, enjoying waterfront views or exclusive amenities. They have access to accommodation close to the city where they work or close to transport. We all know the benefits of owning a house in good locations that allow wealthy people to grow their property value more than in areas where the poor can afford to live.

Savings on early payments or penalties for late payments – The poor miss out on discounts on early payments and oftentimes are penalised for late payments of bills.

Interest – The poor get slapped with interest on credits and loans, while the wealthy get paid interest on their savings and investments. Compounded over a period of many years, this can spell the difference between living wealthy and struggling day to day.

Insurance – In today's world, insurance is a part of life. Living in a poorer suburb makes the poor pay more insurance premiums than those individuals living in wealthier suburbs. Health insurance, CTP Green Slip, comprehensive car insurance, and home and contents insurance premiums are some perfect examples of how expensive it is to be poor.

Assets and personal belongings – Purchasing quality assets, which can last a lifetime, is certainly out of reach for the poor. They would keep buying cheap alternatives and keep replacing them more often than if they bought good-quality assets.

Transport – Mum observed that the poor cannot live close to the city where they work. They oftentimes pay more transport cost because they cannot afford to pay rent close to work. Not only do they spend more money, they also spend more time commuting to work instead of using that precious time to do something else, like rest, spend time with loved ones or pursue hobbies or exercise.

Education – Like my parents' belief, being wealthy gives one an advantage in having access to good-quality education, especially in developing countries where we came from. In the long term, the poor's economic disadvantage may come in the form of limited growth and fewer opportunities.

Lesson 4: It is expensive to be poor. Aim to be a part of the 1 out of 10 instead of the 9 out of 10 millionaire statistic. Learn lessons from poverty and make sure you do not meet again.

5

Human experiences – Redefining wealth

*Those who cannot remember the
past are condemned to repeat it.
– George Santayana*

I underrated myself. I thought we were poor. We were not. We were a work in progress. Even if money was always inadequate, we had abundance in many areas of our lives. Mum and Dad were always positive, and they could reframe situations to give an alternate narrative.

Arellano Avenue

There is so much history in this place. Flood, fire, family, fun.

On Sundays, all of us would be at home because we could not go out, having no money to spend. Mum and Dad would create a fun scenario, pretending that we were boarding a cruise. Marylou would be the captain of the ship, and she would yell, 'All abooooaaard!!'

We would all jump on the queen-sized bed and the single bed, pushed together, and squeeze in and fight for space. Marylou would once again yell, 'We're sailing now. Whoever is not in will be left behind!' We would all hug and cuddle and make sure nobody falls off the pretend boat beds. When someone could not find space and falls off, we catch that person and pull them up, hug one another tighter and rearrange ourselves so all eight of us would fit.

We would pull the bedsheets, in we all went, tickle one another and laugh until Dad says, 'Ok, settle down. It's time to sleep. Boat has left and is now sailing.'

It was so fun!

Mum would say, 'Everything I love is on this boat. We have everything except money. But I love that we don't have money. I love that we're complete and we're all together, hugging one another. We are so blessed, we're here, we're happy, we're healthy, we're safe. Maybe if we had money, everyone would be everywhere, somewhere else. Maybe we're not embracing one another. Maybe this is how God designed our life. We are blessed.'

Some days, we would be baking cassava bread from scratch. Other days, we'd be making potato chips or sweet potato fries or pumpkin fritters. Everyone would be involved in a production line in our small kitchen. We spent so much time preparing these snacks, and we quickly consumed what we made in seconds! Everyone had to be quick. Otherwise, it will quickly run out.

My dad would always joke, 'My family of *enseguida*!' referring to our sense of urgency, that everything should be done quickly. How funny, we even named our pet cat Enseguida – from the Spanish word which means *at once* or *immediately*.

I remember all those amazing Sundays. It was gold. Family love was what carried us through all the years of struggle.

New People's Army in Arellano

One day in mid-1984, my sister, Aldrina, left for her swimming lessons. She had a side hustle of swim coaching at the local YMCA. She left the front door open in her rush. Mum always reminded us to keep the front door locked. As my other sister, Eder, approached to lock the door, realising that Aldrina had already left, the door pulled from the other direction. A man with a gun forced himself inside. He held her close to him, his gun threatening to hurt her.

Panic set in.

Twelve-year-old Eder was only wearing an oversized t-shirt, almost like a night shirt, and undies – probably just woke up. So exposed. So vulnerable. She calmly obeyed the demands of this stranger.

'NPA *ako. Hindi ako pumunta dito para saktan kayo. Kailangan ko lang ng pera at pagkain para sa pamilya ko. Kung bibigyan nyo ako ng pera at alahas, aalis ako ng tahimik. Walang masasaktan,'* he said. ('I'm in the New People's Army (NPA). I did not come here to hurt you. I just need money and food for my family. If you give me money and jewellery, I will walk out quietly. Nobody will get hurt.')

At home was my mum, Eder and our 3-year-old nephew, Charlie. Mum was in total fear and shock. All she could think of was my sister, so exposed in what she was wearing. She could get raped in front of her.

'*Utang na loob, huwag mo saktan ang anak ko. Huwag mo kami saktan,'* Mum cried in plea. '*Wala kaming pera o alahas. Kung gusto mong halughugin ang bahay namin, kunin mo na lahat ng gusto mo. Huwag mo lang siya saktan. Utang na loob, huwag ka gumawa ng gulo.'*

('Please release my daughter. Please don't hurt her. Please don't hurt us.' Mum cried in plea. 'We don't have money or jewellery. If you want to search the whole house, please feel free to search and take whatever you want. Just please don't hurt her. Please do not create trouble.')

Charlie thought it was all an act like a TV show. He jumped out of nowhere and said, 'I am Superman, and I will save all of you.'

The NPA got distracted and pointed the gun at Charlie, enabling Eder to escape from his hold.

'Tumahimik ka diyan. Ikaw ang una kong papatayin,' the NPA said. ('Shut up, or I will kill you first.')

Charlie, now realising that this was a serious situation, began to cry incessantly. Even the NPA was rattled and didn't know what to do. He didn't want the neighbours to be alarmed. Meanwhile, Eder quickly got to the phone to call me at work to ask for help. I quickly rushed home.

Mum settled the situation, sensing that the NPA probably wasn't a murderer or a thief or anything bad. She felt that this man was probably doing this out of destitution. Feeling that the NPA didn't want to escalate the situation further, she prayed loudly. *'Diyos ko, tulungan nyo po ang taong ito. Kung ano man and pinagdadaanan niya, tulungan nyo po kami na tulungan siya.'* ('My God, please help this man. Whatever he is going through, please help us help him.')

The tense situation calmed a little bit, as if the Holy Spirit had descended upon this man.

'Please point the gun at me. I am old. I can die now,' my mum said. 'Please don't hurt the kids. Before that, I will guide you through our entire house. We are poor too. We have no money. We have no expensive jewellery. We have nothing of value, but you can take whatever you want to take. Take our food, take our clothes, take anything. After you get everything, I will kindly escort you outside the door, through the gate and outside the compound until you are out on the street. I will hold your arm as if you were one of my relatives. Nobody, no neighbour will know about this. I promise. Please do not do anything that you will regret forever.'

The NPA began to scour through the house. First, the fridge. When he opened the fridge door, it fell out of place and created a large bang. The hinge was broken. The door was supported by a wooden slab, holding the door from the floor. We would carefully open the door so that the wooden slab would always stay in place and not fall out. But since the NPA didn't know this, he was startled that he might have broken it. Maybe he even felt guilty that he broke it. And upon seeing that there was nothing inside except bottles of water, he left it there.

Next, the cupboards. There were coffee, sugar, salt and old cooking oil, kept to be reused. There were bottles of almost-consumed cheese spread, peanut butter, coco jam. No bread, no eggs, no canned goods, no powdered milk, nothing much. He then started to go upstairs and ransacked through the cabinets of old clothes, boxes of old photos, faded bedsheets, worn-out towels. Upstairs was an old non-functioning TV, old *banig* (handwoven mats) with holes, broken beds, stinking pillows, stained pillowcases and beddings, lots of laundry.

The NPA kept on rummaging through until he realised that my mum was telling the truth: We are also poor. We don't have money. We don't have anything of value.

He asked for water.

My mum kindly gave him a glass of water and said, 'Are you ready to go out? I can escort you now.'

The NPA left empty-handed. Mum, Eder and Charlie were all unhurt.

I arrived just when all the drama had finished.

God has once again blessed this family and this household.

University friends' day out after finals

One day after our final exams at uni, my friends decided to watch a movie to celebrate the end of the term. I begged off, pretending that I was busy at the student council office. I could not go with them because I had no money to pay for a movie ticket and lunch. I wish I could go and have fun. Shame, I hated that we were poor. I always missed out on fun days like this. One of my friends said that she will pay for my movie ticket. Another one said, she'll treat me to lunch. Yet, I said I couldn't join.

I was so sure my mum would be upset if she found out that I went out to the movies with them, had I said yes to my friends. She wouldn't want my friends giving me free stuff.

'Don't be a burden,' she would say. 'If you don't have money, just don't do things you cannot afford.'

My mum always reminded me that I need to focus on my studies. 'Once you finish uni, you can find work. And when you have your own money, you can watch all the movies you want. You can buy all the things that you can afford.'

Mum was always practical. She also taught me independence. 'You need to rely only on yourself. There is no free lunch. No free movie passes,' she said. I was always obedient and did what Mum said.

That night, I received a phone call from one of my friends. They were in the hospital. They weren't able to watch the movie. On their way to the cinema, their car was slowly crossing the intersection when another car, recklessly driving faster than the speed limit, hit them. It was a total wreck. All of them sustained injury, and one of my best friends got seriously hit. She sustained a head injury and possibly needed brain surgery.

My heart sank. It was shocking to hear. My friends were injured, and it could have been me. I could have been this person in the hospital with a head injury. I told my mum about what happened. She had the biggest OMG moment. 'God blesses us in mysterious ways. Let's pray that your friends are ok.'

Married life

Eric and I met at camp during an inter-university leadership training on drug abuse. Both of us were the respective university representatives attending the training. This was our final year of university. We started dating after the camp and got married two years later.

He worked as an operations engineer at the national oil company, and I worked as an accountant in a multinational pharmaceutical.

We started our married life full of dreams and hopes for the future.

We had our first son, who brought so much joy to our families. Our son was the first great-grandson of Eric's grandfather. The fourth-generation male Cardenas was welcomed with so much pride and joy.

We stayed at Eric's family home for three years before we lived on our own. We moved out when we welcomed our second son. This was also the time when Eric decided he would quit his job at the national oil company and establish his own software business.

Placenta previa

In December 1988, Eric and I, together with our 3-year-old son, moved into our rented apartment close to the Makati CBD. It was very conveniently located less than 2 kilometres from my work. I was six months pregnant.

Eric and I have been active members of the gym, and I continued to exercise throughout my pregnancy. The doctor advised that pregnancy is not a disease, and I was encouraged to continue doing what I was physically doing. I used to walk to and from work to exercise, in the belief that this would help me have an easy childbirth. I continued with my healthy routine.

On 4 January 1989, Eric found me early in the morning in the toilet, bleeding profusely, like a valve had malfunctioned, and uncontrollably releasing enormous amounts of blood. I was taken to the nearest hospital, which was a high-end, private hospital about 3 kilometres from home.

I was suffering from placenta previa – a condition wherein the placenta attaches lower in the uterus and covers the cervix, which can be deadly for both the mum and the baby. In a normal, healthy pregnancy, the placenta is positioned above the baby. At childbirth, the placenta should come last, after the baby has been delivered. With my condition, the placenta is positioned to come out before the baby is delivered. I needed a C-section.

There were at least 12 weeks left of my pregnancy. The baby was still very small and nowhere near ready to be delivered. But with every small movement I made, there was bleeding that was affecting both the baby and me. I wanted to transfer to a more affordable hospital, where my ob-gyn was practising. However, with this condition, Eric decided that I should stay in this hospital for a higher chance of delivering a healthy baby and less risk of danger for me.

The doctor advised that I should be a human incubator and stay in the hospital until the day that both the baby and I can hold.

We stayed in the hospital for five weeks, until I could no longer hold. I had to stay in full bed rest the whole time. The doctor advised that I do very minimal movements. I was not allowed to stand up and walk to the toilet. Everything I did was in bed, lying down, just mostly sleeping, eating, drinking and discharging waste. Clean-up was limited to sponge baths and brushing of teeth, with the assistance of a nurse.

By week three, I had developed bedsores and back pains. The extreme discomfort was unbearable, and the bleeding wasn't stopping. The pregnancy was so scary. There's mental torment that, at any time, the baby could be deprived of oxygen, stop breathing and not survive. Or I will not survive from blood loss. Or both of us would leave Eric and my 4-year-old son forever. The emotional strain of being alone in the hospital, separated from my young family, was overwhelming. The stress of not knowing where to get the money to pay the mounting hospital bills was so intense. It was stress all over in all areas – physical, mental, emotional, financial.

I was earning PHP 950 a month then. We had saved up PHP 3,000 for this childbirth. The usual hospital bill for a normal childbirth delivery then was PHP 1,800, and we thought we were well prepared for this one with a little bit of extra. Our hospital bill was already PHP 45,000. Where would we get this amount of money? Worst of all, insurance wouldn't cover this, according to the finest of fine print. Childbirth is not a disease.

On 9 February 1989, an emergency C-section had to be done. My tiny baby boy was born, and he was barely 2 kilograms. His whole foot was half the size of my thumb. His face looked like a new doll manufactured fresh from the toy factory – his eyelids and his mouth weren't open yet. It looked like a stitched-up buttonhole of a new jacket. His pug nose, with a tiny little bump of a nostril, was all just one flat part of his face and had no holes yet. His ears were all scrunched up, still closed like a flower not yet ready to bloom. His little fingers were still all stuck together, still netted like a glued biscuit box with perforations in between that says, 'lift and tear here' and the perforations needed some help to detach. His whole body fit into half my short forearm.

He was taken away to be put in the incubator, his little bed inside looking like a regular dinner plate, where he fit snugly.

He was so small, yet he survived. I survived. We all survived.

Earthquake part 2 and volcanic ashfall

We turned our small apartment into an IT software house. We purchased a few computers and equipment and employed a few programmers. In 1990, my eldest son was 5 years old and my youngest was 18 months.

16 July 1990 was an ordinary day. The programmers were working as usual, Eric was on the road driving to a business meeting, I was at work in our seventh-floor office, and our children were at home with our household helpers, together with our programmers.

At 4:26. pm, an earthquake struck with a magnitude of 7.7 on the Richter scale. Panic set all over the city and within a 250-kilometre radius of the epicentre. At work, we hid under our desks for 45 long seconds of rocking, swaying and shaking of the ground and the building. It felt like forever. There were aftershocks every few minutes, and it seemed to be endless. We could not decide whether to get out from under the desks or run for safety, because it was hard to tell if the earthquake was over or not. The aftershocks were unpredictable and terrifying.

When it was quite safe to escape, we quickly made our way down the building, to the basement carpark, fearing the possible building collapse from the intense movements. It was quite chaotic as everyone in the building was trying to get out at the same time. While driving out of the basement, debris was falling off the side of the glass building, as if the foundation was starting to give way. It was frightening.

On the road, Eric described his drive as if the street was going to split open into many parts. The road was intensely shaking and almost breaking up, as if it were being swallowed into a sinkhole.

He witnessed the swaying of the buildings, the rocking of the cars, the traffic lights in front of him and people in panic running to safety. At home, our children were shocked by the strong sway of the apartment walls and household items and furniture and equipment falling and sliding everywhere.

This earthquake is recorded as the second-deadliest earthquake in the Philippines, with its epicentre around 250 kilometres north of Manila. Among many of the schools, offices and government buildings that collapsed, this earthquake demolished the five-star Hyatt Terraces Hotel like a deck of playing cards. We were there a few months ago, when we attended our national sales conference. It was scary to think that we could be one of the many thousands who perished under the rubble and around the surrounding districts.

But we survived. No harm was done to us.

A year later, on 12 June 1991, halfway between the epicentre of the earthquake and Manila, Mount Pinatubo erupted, spewing lava and volcanic ash. An ash column of 19 kilometres covered the island of Luzon on the first day. On the third day, the seismic activity became more intense, and an ash cloud covered over a radius of 40 kilometres.

Despite being 90 kilometres away from the volcanic ashfall, our little apartment was blanketed by a fine ash cloud. Our white Volkswagen turned brown, as if it were buried by a sandstorm. Even inside our apartment, coarse brown and pink dust covered the surfaces of our furniture and appliances. Apparently, fine ash was spewed as far as the Indian Ocean. According to the US Geological Survey, at least 16 commercial jets inadvertently flew through the drifting ash cloud, sustaining around $100 million in damages.

In the nearby area of Mount Pinatubo, lahar and pyroclastic materials flooded the villages with mud. The roofs of the houses collapsed due to the hot, wet and heavy ashfall. People were trapped inside their homes, and some of the villages were partially buried in hot mud. Around 20,000 people were evacuated, and 10,000 were left homeless.

We were very lucky. We were spared from these catastrophes.

EDSA Revolution

Ninoy Aquino, political opponent of dictatorial President Ferdinand Marcos, was assassinated in August 1983. In February 1986, a snap presidential election was held. It was marred with so many irregularities, fraud and vote manipulation that led to a series of peaceful demonstrations.

My workmate Del and I could not get home on 22 February 1986, caught in the middle of the People Power Revolution. The roads have been blocked; cars and buses were not permitted. Del and I got curious and joined the rally. We walked towards Camp Aguinaldo. Instead of the military protecting the people, it was the people protecting the military trapped inside the camps. People were pleading for justice, for change, for peace, for the Marcos administration to end, for the dictatorship to collapse.

There we were in the middle of the peaceful revolution that went on for hours. A lot of supporters donated food to those joining the peaceful vigils. As some people were distributing food, Del and I queued for macaroni soup packed in clear plastic bags. As we were about to get our share, an active tank started to move. People started to panic. Food was now being thrown instead of being properly handed. As the demonstrators clamoured for food, I got caught in between. A lady near me jumped and reached out for the plastic containing hot macaroni soup, but failed to catch it. Somehow, the pressure from being thrown and her nails piercing the light plastic broke the bag, and the hot macaroni soup, with all its meat, vegetables and thick broth, splattered straight through my hair and face, almost burning my skin.

The People Power Revolution went down in world history as a change of a dictatorial government without violence. But Del and I had another story to tell. Not sure if we were going to laugh or cry, but it was definitely a moment we always recall with a chuckle.

Yes, I survived the hot macaroni soup incident and the People Power Revolution. The next day, my brother was on the front page of all the major newspapers, as he stood bravely in front of all the tanks together with some nuns. My mum was so proud of us being there.

Redundancy from Rhône-Poulenc Rorer

In July 1991, my position at Rhône-Poulenc Rorer was made redundant. During this time, Manila was experiencing intensive electricity power failures. Sometimes there would be blackouts for 8 to 16 hours during the day.

Our little software business was greatly affected. We had programmers coming in to work but could not do anything because there was no power. They were sitting around all day doing nothing, and we could not meet the deadlines for our projects. It was difficult in terms of operating costs. We had to pay wages, yet we could not bill our clients for not delivering the software programs on time. Our business was running on deficit.

Being made redundant was a blessing, in a way, because my severance pay could cover the operating costs while we were waiting for projects to be completed and billed. However, we could not keep going like this. We installed an uninterrupted power supply (UPS), so when the electricity gets cut off, the programmers could keep working. However, the blackouts became more regular and lasted for longer periods of time – even the UPS could not be charged long enough to provide backup power. It was a big issue for our small business.

My redundancy payout started to be depleted, so Eric and I wound down the business. We prayed that something better would happen. We advised his employees to seek opportunities outside of our small software house, and they soon found work in bigger organisations. One staff member was taken by one of our clients as their senior programmer. The blackouts continued, and it was not sustainable for us to keep operating. Sadly, we had to close shop.

In the meantime, Marylou needed someone to bring her 4-year-old daughter back to the US. She was being cared for by her husband's sister in Manila. They took her on a holiday, but circumstances have changed and they could no longer take her back. She needed to be accompanied by an adult when going back to the US, so my mum asked me if I could take my niece.

In Manila, applying for a US visa was a very difficult process. People used to queue up as early as 4 am to secure a place in line, long before the embassy opens its doors. There were so many documents required – bank statements, work certificates, business connections, itinerary, health certificates and many more. A few of my friends and relatives have been denied a tourist visa, failing to prove their intention to return to Manila after their visit. Even with work-related travel and sponsorship, US visas are still denied if the applicant fails to convince the consul that they are worthy of being issued a US visa. It's almost like a golden ticket from Charlie and the Chocolate Factory.

I was granted a tourist visa, and I was so happy. It was an opportunity for me to take a break while I was processing too many things in my head – my redundancy, our business closing down, my next steps going forward.

I took my niece to LA to join her mum, Marylou. While in the US, we did the touristy stuff – visit San Francisco, go to Las Vegas, enjoy LA, catch up with friends and family. It was an enjoyable experience, but I was missing Eric and the kids. I was thinking about what to do after the novelty wore off. Marylou said I should look for employment opportunities in the US since I was already there and that I should apply for a working visa with the intention of eventually being able to petition my family.

I seriously considered her advice, but it was very hard for me to make a decision without Eric. On the same day I was thinking of him, he called me. At that time, an overseas phone call was very, very expensive, so we needed to make it brief. We had to plan what we had to say, say it quickly and make sure we understood each other so we don't spend too much money on the phone call. It should be a transactional conversation; no small talk of missing each other or details of how the kids are doing or any form of emotions involved.

While I was feeling anxious and uncertain, Eric was so excited and happy! He wasn't doing a quick transactional phone call as I expected. There was a lot of 'I hope you are having a great time there. The kids are fine here. We're missing you so much, but not long now.'

What's going on? He excitedly shared the news – he received a letter from the Australian Embassy that our application for migration had been approved. A few months before my redundancy, we applied for a permanent residence visa in Australia, and now we are given a maximum of six weeks to leave! What a blessing!

My anxiety turned into excitement and then into gratitude. I cried tears of joy. It was as if there was an invisible force, a virtual manager somewhere in the universe, and everything was organised for us. An unfolding of the divine order!

The timing couldn't be more perfect. The business had wound down, the employees had been settled, we'd finalised all the business taxes, I'd taken my niece to the US, I was done with my unexpected holiday break, Eric had finished all his projects – it was time to move on. Even our apartment was at the end of its lease. And now, here came the next steps that we were praying for! It was totally amazing.

I went home to Manila. In a matter of five weeks, we were able to organise our trip to Sydney, packed whatever belongings we could fit in our maximum allowable limit of eight balikbayan boxes, disposed of all other furniture, appliances and personal belongings, and said goodbye to family and friends.

We went home to my mum and dad's hometown in Lopez, Quezon, to my grandma's tomb to say our last goodbyes. We weren't sure if and when we would be back again. We saw our uncles, aunties and cousins in the province. We were even able to organise a farewell dinner in Manila to bid our families and friends farewell.

The most amazing thing was we still had left over money from my redundancy, which was our safety net once we arrived in Australia, so we weren't empty-handed.

Lesson 5: Trust in God's divine timing. It's never a question of "if" but "when" – Joy Marino

6

Life in Australia

Life is about change. Sometimes it's painful.
Sometimes it's beautiful. But most of the time it's both.
– Kristin Kreuk

We arrived in Australia in 1991 with our two small children. With our educational qualifications, work experience, English-speaking skills, family sponsorship and support from my most generous aunt and uncle, Eric and I were fortunate to be granted visas as permanent residents of Australia.

It was exciting and, at the same time, very sad, daunting and scary. Although we speak English well, Australian English was quite different from the English we knew. There were new words that we heard for the first time, and there's the Aussie accent that made it extra difficult. On top of this, there's an Aussie sense of humour and friendly sarcasm unknown to us that they use in their everyday language. It was very intimidating for new migrants.

It took a long time for us to settle because we could not find work in our areas of expertise. Most workplaces were looking for local experiences, which, of course, we didn't have because we had just arrived. We also arrived during the worst time in Australia – the recession. 'The recession we (Australians) had to have', as per Paul Keating's famous words.

Even those with local experience had lost their job. We were competing with workers who had been made redundant, those with years of local experience and whose English skills include speaking and understanding local lingo and Aussie accent, humour and sarcasm.

My aunty and her family were so kind, generous and supportive every step of the way. My aunt is my dad's sister, and she reminds me so much of him – just as kind and generous. All my grandma's children are like that – gentle, kind and generous. That's just how they are and how they were raised by Grandma.

Aunty is one of those church ladies, always supporting everyone. She arrived in Australia with her family in the late '70s. Together with her husband, they founded the Filipino Catholic Organisation of Sydney (FilCOS). They were very active members of the Filipino community through this organisation. They introduced us to their many friends, most of whom were nurses and tradesmen who arrived when Australia just ended its long-held white policy. They were among the first non-White migrants who answered Australia's call for multiculturalism in the late '60s. Most of them held jobs in the factory, post office and hospitals, doing menial or mechanical work.

They advised us to take any kind of work to survive – apply for a cleaning job or a sorter at the post office or a factory hand or a 'peter and turner'. We didn't even know what a 'peter and turner' is. Filipinos are known for exchanging f's and p's in our words. It's a local humour only Filipinos understand and laugh about. Apparently, 'peter and turner' is actually 'fitter and turner' – a real job in some manufacturing plants. We arrived in late November, very close to Christmastime. Leading up to Christmas, there were no jobs available, so it was very difficult to find work.

The Filipino network of my aunt and uncle loves to celebrate. From our arrival in late November through to Christmas and towards the new year, there were so many celebrations – birthday lunches, anniversary dinners, weekend BBQs, weekday church novena and weeknight catch-ups. It was not something we were used to. We rarely got invited to events when we were in the Philippines, but here in Sydney, it was wonderful. We didn't get homesick during this period because everyone was friendly, warm and hospitable. Filipinos are also known for our warm hospitality. Everyone took turns in taking us everywhere, as if we were tourists.

We went as a big group to tour the Sydney Opera House, Darling Harbour and city centre, rode the Tangara train, took the monorail, went up to Sydney Tower, and walked around the city in true touristy style. On weekends, we were treated to Bondi Beach, a trip to Wollongong, a fishing and oyster-picking trip and a trip to Canberra. One day, my aunt took us to Waratah Park, where we saw kangaroos and koalas for the first time. We took a train ride inside the park; it was totally amazing! The kids were overwhelmed by all the trips that we never experienced in Manila.

On Christmas Eve, Christmas Day, New Year's Eve and New Year's Day, the celebrations galore continued. We were invited from one house to another. Each host gave us presents we so undeserved. It was an unbelievably warm welcome. The kids got lots of toys and clothes for Christmas, and we got lots of stuff for the house, as if it were a bridal shower for a newly married couple.

Everyone was so warm and welcoming. This is our new home now, with a beautiful, supportive network of new aunts and uncles from different grandparents.

Come the new year of 1992, life began. Everyone went back to work, and the normal set in. No more parties and no more touristy day outs and weekends away. We were on our own to get our new life in Australia started. We were looking for work that we had qualifications for. We believed that Australia accepted us as migrants based on our education, skills and work experience. We continued to look for work opportunities and went to Commonwealth Employment Services (CES), which is now known as Centrelink, for support. We were eligible to apply for family benefits with dependents and as new migrants.

One month on, after hundreds of job applications sent and unsuccessful letters received, we began to feel the stress of our new life in Australia.

Two months. Still no positive response.

Three months. Four months – still the same.

The human spirit began to break and then doubts its capacity to fight and go on. Is this really a good decision to leave our lives in Manila for this? How long can we keep going like this? Will we ever find work in Australia?

My supportive aunty had all the encouraging words to keep going. 'Just pray. I'm here for you all the time,' she always reminded us. I can feel, though, that we were being a burden on her family.

In her house, she had 21 and 18-year-old daughters, a 5-year-old son and a husband. Plus us – Eric, our 6-year-old son, our terrible

2-year-old toddler and me. My aunt asked his two older sons (25 years old and 23 years old) to move out to look after their grandpa, my aunt's father-in-law. They lived in another house 200 metres away.

My mum, in the meantime, kept reminding me to leave my aunt's house and find our own accommodation. 'Don't be a burden to anyone. Be independent. Don't abuse the kindness of your aunt.'

I knew what my mum meant. There were way too many people in my aunt's house. Everyone had their own character, behaviour, moods, beliefs, values, idiosyncrasies. It would be quite challenging. No matter how good people are – call it compassionate, kind, tolerant, patient, understanding – living with too many adults under one roof can cause dysfunction.

Mum would always remind me not to overstay. 'Aunty has done great things for you. Do not overextend your stay. Just leave now. Do not wait until your relationship is strained before you make a decision to leave. Do not wait until you get booted out of their house. Make sure you leave their house on good terms.'

My mum was very wise. She knew human behaviour so well. I think I inherited a lot of that from her. My aunty will never ever do what my mum was thinking, though. In fact, she wanted us to stay with her for as long as possible. She would often tell me, 'Stay with us for as long as possible. Save your rent money for a house deposit. When the time comes that you are ready for a home mortgage, move out to your own home.'

My aunt never asked for a single cent for rent or to contribute to household expenses. Even if I asked her how much a good amount to contribute, she would always say, 'No. Don't do that. You need it more than I do. Keep it and save it.'

Eric was quite confused. He came from a family that is upfront. When we stayed with them in our early years, his mum would say, 'Your contribution to our household is PHP 1,500 a month.' That's them. They had clear lines. Everything was transactional.

I encouraged Eric that we leave my aunty's house, but he refused. He was a very pragmatic person. He said, 'We don't have work, and you want us to move out of Aunty's place? Here we get free rent, food, support. Aunty will be upset if we move out. She might think that we are proud and arrogant, trying to prove that we are independent, even if we know we will not survive without her help.'

He was wrong. Mum was right. We should not have overextended and abused Aunty's kindness. We should just trust and pray that by God's grace, everything will be fine, that we would be able to make do with what we are given. After a few discords and minor misunderstandings, we decided to move out. The minor conflicts and clashes in family subculture and values somehow put some strain on our relationship.

We were adjusting to our new environment. In Manila, the boys had *yayas* (au pairs) who help them with their everyday needs. We had household help to do the daily chores – laundry, ironing, cooking, cleaning and grocery. Here, we had no one. We had to do these chores. In fact, we had to do some extra house chores to help out Aunty. This was the right thing to do because we were not even paying board. We needed to carry our weight and not be a burden.

Meanwhile, my aunt's family was also struggling. They were used to being a household by themselves. Suddenly, there were four extra heads to deal with. Their fridge was suddenly packed with food that was not theirs. Using the laundry and shower now needed to be scheduled. The food I cooked was not what they wanted. Little things like these can be annoying. I felt bad because I didn't want to disrupt their otherwise peaceful family before we arrived.

My aunty continued to be kind to us and assured us that she was always here for us. We remained close with them. She treated me like her own daughter, and I treated her as my second mum.

By the fifth month, and by God's grace, I was able to secure a job. We had moved into the cheapest unit in Fairfield, close to the train station, shops and childcare.

I found work in finance in a computer company located in St Leonards, 40 kilometres north of Sydney. This was really far for me; my work in Manila was only 5 kilometres away. But I didn't care. I had a job. No place was far. I desperately needed a job. I needed to restart my career somewhere.

My cousin, Aunt's oldest son, had the heart of his mum. He worked close to St Leonards and offered to give me a lift every day. He was such a godsend, making my daily commute a pleasure as we shared stories, talked and laughed in the car about family matters.

I was actually surprised that I got a job in my line of work. The oldies were asking me to apply for work as a cleaner or in McDonald's or as a check-out chick in the local Franklins. I actually applied for work in these areas but was told that I was overqualified. Shame.

HR interviewed me and asked me if I was willing to take an IQ test. I was really happy to take an IQ test. Without a local experience, it was my chance to prove that I can work in finance or admin, which I had been doing for the last 10 years in Manila. When I was invited for a final interview, the manager told me that they were impressed by my score in the IQ test, that's why they were offering me the job.

The job was just an admin assistant. I was wondering why an IQ test was required, but I was happy. I finally broke into the job market. From an admin assistant, I eventually moved up to finance when the finance manager found out I had experience in finance as a CPA.

Microsoft

More months had passed, and still no work for Eric. It was hard on my part. He tried to make use of his time by getting to know people outside of my aunty's circle. He played basketball and ping pong, and went to the gym, as he would when we were in Manila. He continued to receive acknowledgement letters that said his application for the position was received but was unsuccessful.

One uncle who was working at Aeroplane Jelly told him that if Eric was interested in a casual job, he could help him. For a couple of weeks, he worked in Aeroplane Jelly on the manufacturing packaging floor. He was later let go because of low production forecasts. Also, he wasn't good and efficient enough on the packaging floor.

Six months. Still no luck.

Seven months. Nothing.

He was starting to get depressed.

Although I had fulltime work, I was also the main person managing the kids and the household. He was not used to helping with house chores in Manila, so he just watched TV, went to the gym and played basketball and ping pong. I never asked him to help with the housework and let him do whatever he wanted to help with his situation. I felt like he was starting to doubt himself and his capabilities. On top of my fulltime work, kids and house duties, I needed to support him emotionally. It was tough on me.

After seven months and hundreds of application letters sent, he noticed the pattern of why he could not get work – he didn't have any local experience! But how could he have any if nobody would accept him and give him a local experience? Please give him a chance.

He decided he was going to work for free (volunteer work) just to get local experience. He was accepted as a volunteer all-rounder in Computron, an IT training provider. He worked there for a couple of months until the manager spoke to him.

'We can no longer take you in as a volunteer. The union laws disallow us from doing this. We cannot have someone who is not being compensated work for us. You have to leave. I can refer you to my friend who owns a small business. Maybe he can offer you something.'

Prayer was always the strength that carried us through. Every night, my boys and I would pray. My little miracle placenta previa baby would fervently pray, 'God, please help my dad find work.' Eric would not be there to pray with us. Though he is a spiritual person, he finds his strength in different ways. One day, my son said, 'Dad, maybe if you prayed with us, God will help you find work.'

That night, it struck him. It had been eight months – too long not to have paid work. As if the Holy Spirit descended upon him, in all humility, he bowed down in prayer with us. 'Thy will be done, O Lord. Please help me find what is mine.'

Submission. He finally submitted himself to God's plan. We always believed that if God deprived us of something, it was for the purpose of giving us something better.

In a matter of days, we received a call from a headhunter, saying they have a client who needed a person with the unique skills of Fox Base, a database we had used in our small software business in Manila. They couldn't find anyone with that knowledge, skill and experience. *Voila!* They were talking to the right person – Eric. Their client was Microsoft!

In a few weeks, he was employed at Microsoft. What a dream come true! We never imagined that in all that waiting, God had something huge waiting for us. That was a new beginning of our life-changing journey.

Lesson 6: God's timing is perfect. He orchestrates events in our lives according to His Divine plan.

7

Lifestyle choices – Simplicity

In character, in manner, in style . . .
the supreme excellence is simplicity
– Henry Wadsworth Longfellow

If there is something that works very well between Eric and me, it is living a life of honesty, practicality, communication and simplicity. He is almost the complete opposite of my dad. I must have subconsciously chosen him so that I don't repeat my mum's experiences. In contrast to my dad, Eric does not drink alcohol, does not smoke, does not gamble, is not charming and is not the life of the party, likes to take care of his body through exercise, likes to play sports, loves to watch TV, enjoys music and likes to do his own thing.

The opposite of all that is my dad. But both of them are generous and loving in their own ways.

One of the things that frustrated my mum throughout their marriage was that Dad never allowed her to manage the family budget, not that he didn't trust her. It was because there was always never enough. Dad was not regularly employed. Sometimes he had work, sometimes he didn't. He hated to say and accept that he was an eight-to-five employee. That was his pride – always asserting that he was a consultant, that's why he did not have a regular income. But when he was paid consultancy fees, he would splurge. Dad loved to spend money like there was so much to spend. His financial literacy sucked. He was very generous to family and friends, even if he had nothing.

My mum is the one who had a naturally high financial IQ. She was really good with money. Dad was so bad with money. Mum never knew how much Dad's earnings were. He would be very upset if we talked about money or asked about how much he earned. He always said that it was rude to talk about money, that it was not good breeding to speak of money. It was a total taboo to talk about money in our house; don't ever dare.

Client case:

Female, 32 years old, married, no dependent, with mental health issues, unemployed but is trying to find work. Husband has fulltime work. She wants to see me because she believes that they have financial troubles, but she is unclear about it. She wants to speak to her husband about buying things at home and discuss their financial situation. Each time she tries to discuss money, it ends in an argument.

For many years, growing up, I believed my dad that money should not be discussed. I didn't want to upset him or be judged as rude. We never talked about money. As a financial counsellor, I learned that the topic of money should not be vague. It is ok to discuss money within the context of financial literacy and financial planning.

One thing about financial success between couples is that it is a joint effort and commitment. When I see clients who are going through financial hardship simply because, as a couple, they could not communicate properly or are not honest and open with each other, I remember my mum and dad. They did not talk about money. It was a taboo. They had no long-term plans or strategies. There was no transparency. We call it *bahala na* attitude – meaning, whatever happens, happens. Just trust that things will work out without any intent of financial success.

Money issues are a main cause of relationship breakdown. If not properly mitigated, it can cause stress and unpleasant outcomes. Couples can have mismatched financial priorities, poor financial literacy, lack of communication and financial infidelity, such as hiding purchases or secret debts. Most of the time, couples may earn significantly different amounts of money, and there is an unequal contribution towards the family fund. This must be managed through proper communication to avoid power imbalance and avoid insecurity and resentment or any cause of argument.

I've seen different ways people manage their finances together as a couple, both in my practice and within my own circle of family and friends. There aren't a lot of couples who manage their finances using a joint account. While having a joint account can be daunting for some people, having to give up control and freedom, it is one of the best ways to efficiently manage family finances and achieve financial goals.

I've observed couples having so many accounts between them – separate individual accounts, his and hers accounts, joint accounts, business accounts and some secret accounts. Some bills are paid by one partner, and another partner pays something else. Someone may be in charge of groceries and utilities, while the other may be in charge of paying the home mortgage. They can independently earn and spend money on whatever they want to buy.

While it all gets too confusing for me in our very simple approach to life, I respect that some couples can work around their own system of managing their money.

In my practice, I find that couples usually get in trouble because they are not financially aware of what is happening until something really bad happens. What if the other partner falls permanently ill and can no longer work? What if the partner paying the home loan dies? So many times, I'm seeing clients where the partner, usually the wife, does not have a clue what to do because the husband, who is in charge of everything, has fallen ill or has suddenly passed away. Some clients don't even know the financial details (bank account, superannuation, insurance, investments) of their partner.

One of my biggest tips for couples to achieve financial independence and success is trust. If you cannot trust each other with money, expect complexities in achieving your financial goals, which are directly related to your relationship goals. Fix your relationship goals to fix your financial goals.

Eric and I are both open to talking about anything, most especially about money. We like to keep things simple, easy and transparent. We trust that both of us are doing our absolute best for our family. We both believe that money touches every aspect of our lives, and we respect and work around this belief system.

The life we live is easy because we intentionally do not complicate things. We buy things only if we can afford them. We eat healthy food, prioritising our health and wellbeing. We have long-term goals. In terms of money management, all our accounts are joint in both our names for ease of management. We have one bank account, one credit card and a few investment accounts – all in both our names.

Since the beginning of our relationship, all income has gone into one account. We use our credit card for all expenses to gain points and to track our spending. We pay our credit card in full on the due date to avoid paying interest. We set a limit of a certain amount, say $500. If we have to spend on a personal item, we talk about it and we make a joint decision.

We used to have a budget sheet to jot down every single item we spent, large or small, no exception – groceries, transport, electricity bill, rent, phone, childcare, chocolate from the petrol station, donations, medical insurance, car expenses, among others. We did this for the purpose of tracking down our expenses. Writing down things gave us the awareness of where our money went. We had a purpose for doing this, aiming for long-term financial independence.

We don't do that anymore. It became like muscle memory, and when we were comfortable with creating a regular surplus in our budget, we researched our savings and investment strategies.

To build our investment portfolio, we aimed to save $10,000 periodically and invest in lump sum. During those days, investment was not as easy as today, where you can build up your nest egg by depositing small amounts regularly and benefiting from dollar cost averaging. Two to three decades ago, there was a minimum amount to invest. We aimed to save $10,000 at a time – whether it took us 12 months, six months or three months to do this, we had a target. Like a regular chore, we would review our statement of financial position periodically.

We also saved for depreciating assets, like a car. We would never buy a car if we couldn't afford to pay for it in cash. We figured out early on that **interest expense** is a very costly item on the budget, but **interest income** is our friend. We would use interest to our advantage when purchasing a depreciating asset.

If we needed to purchase a car, the $10,000 savings would go to a separate short-term time deposit account, and not to our long term investment account. We would create a few short-term time deposits until we have enough money to purchase a car in cash. This strategy enabled us to get to our target financial goal quicker by using the power of interest income on our side.

We created separate term deposits instead of putting the $10,000 in our long-term investment account because we believed that the $10,000 in a short-term time deposit was a safe choice to protect the savings from short-term market fluctuations. We knew that before the end of the 18th month, we would have saved up for the new car. Upon maturity, we would be ready to purchase a brand new car.

We also found out that we could negotiate for a better deal when purchasing in cash. For example, the car dealership would throw in some free stuff like car mats, tints, paint and upholstery protection, car registration, premium car plates, and more, saving us thousands of dollars.

All these add up.

Lesson 7: Embrace simplicity. Focus on what truly matters to find joy. Enrich life with love, harmony and fulfillment.

8

Family relationships – Opposite of simple

Ohana means family. Family means
nobody gets left behind or forgotten.
– Lilo and Stitch

Family is very important to us. No matter how simple we choose our lifestyle to be, we get involved with family matters outside of our own backyard.

Prayer request for a son

My brother was the apple of my parents' eyes. He was the only son among six children. My mum tells the story that they have always wanted to have a son to carry on the family surname. Dad was the eldest son in the family, and it was really important for him to have a son – it is like a sense of pride and joy that he is able to give his mum a grandson, the ultimate give-back to a mother.

My parents' first two children were girls, whom they adored so much, but they wanted their next child to be a boy. My mum said that she prayed the novena and kneel-walked from the main entrance to the altar of Quiapo Church, a well known minor Basilica and national shrine of Jesus Nazarene in Manila, to ask for a boy while she was heavily pregnant. Kneel-walking is a common scene in Quiapo Church, as millions of devotees demonstrate suffering, faith, hope and love to the Black Nazarene, known and believed to be miraculous and grants prayer requests and special wishes.

My mum had her prayers answered, and she delivered a baby boy. They were very happy that, finally, the family lineage would not be broken. There is an heir to the Z clan. Unfortunately, the baby was unhealthy. He had a rare disease that the doctors could not diagnose. He probably had an allergy that was still unknown in the 1960s. He could not take mother's milk or infant formula made from cow's milk, and his skin was peeling off. Mum described my baby brother's skin as raw, wet and constantly seeping with pus. He was very sensitive.

Mum felt so sorry that she asked for a son. This was her prayer request. In her heart, she thought it was punishment for her because she had asked for a son instead of a healthy child. Maybe she was granted a son, but in return, her son would suffer a medical condition in his lifetime. As a very prayerful person, she felt that she had the wrong prayer. She thought she should just be happy with what she was given. She blamed herself for my brother's medical condition. My poor mum. My poor baby brother.

She went back to Quiapo Church. Once again, she kneel-walked from the entrance to the altar, asked for forgiveness, asked for any form of punishment for her, just for my brother to be healthy, and said, 'Thy will be done, oh Lord.'

Through trial and error, the doctors finally found a special infant formula made from goat's milk that would suit my brother. He eventually outgrew his medical condition and lived a normal childhood. My mum went back to Quiapo Church, kneel-walked and expressed her fervent gratitude. She swore, from now on, never to ask for anything that is not of God's will.

My brother grew up with skin allergies and asthma. He became this precious, favourite child of Mum and Dad. He had special treatment all the time and would be exempt from house chores. He would be favoured when sibling rivalry arises. He had special, yummy food that we all craved for but was only reserved for the special one.

Mum would always say, 'This food is for your brother only. He has a special condition and has a special dietary requirement.'

All these happened even when my brother was no longer showing symptoms of his condition.

My mum was fair. Even if she favoured my brother most times, she would still get frustrated with him when he plays up, as all little boys do. She would often say, 'Girls are easier to discipline. But this boy, it's hard work sometimes.'

She was quite funny when, oftentimes, when at wits' end with my naughty brother, she would say, 'If only I knew you would grow up like this – so hard-headed, so difficult to discipline, so naughty – I wouldn't have kneel-walked in Quiapo Church. I am being punished for doing this.'

My dad and my brother had a special bond that we girls didn't enjoy with Dad. They would play chess together all the time, and Dad would take him to special events. One time, they went on an out-of-town trip together. They showed us pictures of them having a picnic and my brother enjoying a horse ride in a camp. It was a male thing.

My dad and brother's bond grew stronger in adulthood. They became drinking buddies and shared their life experiences as if they were best friends. Dad was very proud of my brother. He was very handsome, smart and popular in school. He was active in the Catholic Association at his university; he even became president. Dad opened his most precious wine bottle the night my brother was declared president. My brother's friends were all there to cheer them both. Dad was always there to support my brother, and my brother was always there to support my dad.

My dad and mum immigrated to the US in 1990 to join Marylou. Little did we know, Dad left a secret with my brother – a secret that both of them sacredly held.

Father and son gentlemen's agreement

In some ways, my brother was like my dad – maybe 80% of my dad. He was very outgoing, had great energy, brought life to a party, was very popular with the ladies. He was as charming as Dad.

My brother had a colourful love life. On his wedding day, drama unfolded when his ex-girlfriend created a bloody scene and stabbed my brother with a knife, trying to steal him from his bride. It was an if-I-can't-have-you-no-one-can situation. We often talk about it now with candour and humour that he was such a heartthrob, even on his wedding day, blood would flow. Fortunately, it was an unsuccessful attempt at murder. My sister-in-law had accepted that she was the lucky one; he married her. She was deeply smitten and vowed to love him forever, regardless of his imperfections.

My brother was a dedicated husband to his wife and father to his five children. However, he would sometimes indulge in 'silly' things that would leave my sister-in-law doubting if there was any third party involved.

One day, in the early 2000s, she noticed that there was missing money in their budget. When asked, my brother would make excuses as to where the money went. As the suspicions grew and with evidence of the continuing missing money, my sister-in-law made her own investigations.

One day, she secretly followed my brother, who went to a house around 15 kilometres south of Manila. She watched closely as he knocked on the gate and a lady opened it. My brother dropped off an envelope and left.

My sister-in-law supposed that the envelope contained cash. As he did not even enter the gate, she got confused. If this were a third-party person, wouldn't he be invited to go inside, at least for a drink? That night, when she confronted him, he denied any wrongdoing, saying he was just doing an errand for someone but would not disclose any further details.

As my sister-in-law was the patient, quiet, peaceful type of person, she tried to erase any suspicions, even if she was still upset from the missing money that their children badly needed. In her pain and frustration, she spoke to my mum about my brother. She cried and said that if this goes on and she could prove that there is a third party, she would have to leave her husband.

My mum consoled my sister-in-law and asked for more patience and understanding for the sake of their children. Mum asked her to be strong and shared some of her pain with Dad in her younger days. She said that this will all pass. Men go through some of these phases. All will be ok in the end. Just hang in there.

Mum, with her unique sense of humour, even joked that since she was poor and no inheritance could be expected from her, she would like my sister-in-law to take this similar storyline as an inheritance instead.

'Ikaw ang tagapagmana ko ng sama ng loob. 'Yan lang ang maipamamana ko sa iyo. Ikaw lang, wala ng iba,' Mum said. ('You are the sole beneficiary of my hardships and emotional pain. That is the only inheritance I can leave you. Only for you, no one else.')

My mum developed a deep sense of bond with my sister-in-law. She loved her immensely – sometimes, more than her real daughters – that she can joke about inheritance with her but not with her girls. We would often hear Mum say this, and we would always laugh about it that she is the chosen lucky one to have 100% and we don't want any part of that inheritance, as instructed by Mum.

The days passed. The missing money stopped missing. Everything went back to normal, but the mystery stayed in the background.

50th wedding anniversary of Mum and Dad

Wedding anniversaries are important to us. Every year, we would celebrate Mum and Dad's wedding anniversary, no matter how small or how simple. We could just pray the rosary or attend church together, and that would be our celebration.

In 2003, my mum and dad celebrated their 50th wedding anniversary and had a grand event in Manila. It was great. We rented a hotel venue and dressed up in gold and white formal attire. It was my cousin priest's first mass after his recent ordination. What a blessing to have Father Benjamin celebrate Mum and Dad's renewal of vows as his first mass as a fully ordained priest. It came full circle as Mum and Dad supported him through his journey to priesthood.

Many of our cousins, uncles, aunties and friends were invited. A lot came from our province and overseas to join in the celebration. Uncle Manny, my dad's older cousin and best friend, spoke well of the many years he witnessed their relationship, since day one. He joked about how Dad was a chick magnet, was so charming and always the life of the party, but in the end, he would always come back home to the arms of Mum. Lots and lots of fun and laughter with family and friends brought together in this celebration of life and love.

It was a wonderful, memorable event for all of us. My parents travelled back to San Francisco after this. As it would happen, an earthquake of a different kind would rock our family after this great event. Back in San Francisco, my mum, while cleaning up, randomly found a birth certificate of a Liezel Ann Zamora. *Mother: Eliza Ortega, signed. Father: Benjamin Zamora, signed.* My dad.

My poor mum. After a grand celebration of love, commitment and years of sacrifice, this is what she discovered – my dad had a love child outside their marriage. The mystery unfolded, and the truth was revealed.

It was such a painful experience for all of us, especially for my mum. She worked so hard to get to where she is right now, dreaming of a retirement of travel and a good life. Then this. How can Dad do such a thing? So much betrayal.

It was as if the joke was on her. The mystery of the missing money from my sister-in-law's storyline has now been solved. My brother was protecting a gentleman's agreement he had with my dad. My brother knew my dad's secret! Dad told him that he had a love child long before my sister-in-law had suspicions of a third party. My supportive brother had promised Dad that he was not going to tell anyone about this – not Mum, not his wife, not any of his siblings. But now, they've both been busted. There is no telling lies any more. Everything was clear and made sense. They confessed. The truth was revealed.

Dad was trying to support his love child the best he could. He used to work odd, casual jobs in Walmart and Ross. In times when he was short of cash, he would ask my brother to send some money to Liezel Ann and her mum to provide some form of support. Those are the times when my brother would dig into their family budget and provide something for Dad's love child.

Shame on my dad. Shame on my brother. How can this happen?

Mum left Dad in San Francisco, so confused. She didn't know what to do. First, she went back to the Philippines, closed all their joint accounts and organised her own financials. She arranged to meet up with Liezel Ann and her mum to understand and know their status.

She was so upset, confused, hurt, angry, overwhelmed, lost, betrayed – all the unpleasant emotions combined. That's how she felt. My mum is a very strong woman. We never saw her sick when we were growing up – either she kept all her pains to herself, or she was just really healthy and strong. We never saw her shed a tear. She never showed weakness of spirit in any situation. She seemed like she was always in control.

Side story: I spoke to two of my good friends from high school and shared this story. I visited my friend in France, and she told me that the same thing happened to her mum, that she found out that her dad had a mistress. Her mum passed away from a heart attack after a few weeks, not being able to take the emotional burden. I went to Los Angeles to visit another friend, and she told me that they also had their dad betray them. They had a playmate who was their piano teacher's son. Later on, they found out that he was their dad's son with their piano teacher! Months later, their mum had a stroke after such a discovery and was ill for a very long time. So when I told them my version, they really admired my mum, saying that she's such a strong woman to be able to bear this.

But Mum's way to release stress was through anger. She would find a reason when we do something wrong and pick on us in the guise of responsible parenting, discipline and tough love. We coped with it. But this time, her vulnerability finally appeared. She went to Uncle Manny, and she cried her heart out. She cried and cried and cried until she could no longer cry. Many years of heartache, pain and sacrifice flowed like a river. All of Uncle Manny's wonderful words during the grand 50th wedding anniversary celebration were reduced to nothing now. My poor mum.

Mum's rage and catharsis

My mum asked my sister-in-law and Eder to take her to meet 14-year-old Liezel Ann. They organised a meeting at a Chowking fast-food chain. Mum was always meek and never argumentative. She did not like discussing things. She wasn't very comfortable being open and friendly with neighbours or church friends. At school, we knew that if we did something wrong, she would not be there to support us; we were on our own. When we had parent–teachers night, she would never attend. She always had an excuse not to attend. She could not speak to any teacher or any person of authority. Not because she didn't want to, but because she didn't have the confidence to do so. Especially in the private school that we attended, she felt out of place. She would never be in the same room with those rich parents. She never wanted any confrontation of any kind. She had this inferiority complex, leaving everything to Dad when it came to speaking to or confronting people or having to explain things or presenting her side of an argument or simply sorting things out. It was like a power distance she developed over the years that Dad was the powerful one who could talk, and she was just a subservient wife who did what she was told.

With her children, her style was to always use us to vent what was boiling inside her, find something minor we did or did not do, and release on us whatever frustration she was experiencing. We would cope with every single rage inside her, as if we were her catharsis. We learned early on to always be at our best behaviour to avoid unnecessary violence. Her inferiority complex did not allow her to express herself with an equal or someone with authority. In fact, it was only us, her children, whom she would treat like this. No one else. She never had the confidence to say or do anything to anyone.

But today she treated Leizel Ann as her own child, her catharsis.

She met Liezel Ann and irresponsibly unleashed on her all her anger for Dad, as if she was a chopping board to take in all the blame. This poor child.

Three adult women in a Chinese restaurant with a 14-year-old girl still in her school uniform, my mum leading them. What a scene! Mum said hurtful words and blamed her.

'Do you know that you are taking food out of the mouths of my grandchildren?' she started, referring to my brother's children. 'My son had to give you money instead of spending it on his children. You are being a burden to his family, do you know that? Who do you think you are? How dare you call my husband Papa? Do you know who your Papa is? He's a poor, nasty, old, irresponsible man. Don't ever think your Papa is coming back for you. Forget about your Papa. Don't ever ask for money from my son or your Papa ever again.'

Shocked and confused, poor innocent Liezel Ann cried and cried from the abusive words. Eder told me that it was the most heartbreaking scene in her life. While she understood what Mum was going through, she felt injustice for Liezel Ann. It wasn't fair. She was also our sister. She didn't deserve this. She didn't ask to be born. She was equally a victim.

She was so brave to front the three adults, and out of nowhere, this was how she was treated. From that moment on, Eder decided to do the right thing for her.

Mum realised how out of character the behaviour she demonstrated was. She was also hurt and felt guilty for what she had done and all the hurtful words she had said. After all, she was a church lady. Church ladies don't do and say nasty things like this. She asked Liezel Ann to calm down and order any food that she wanted, realising that the girl must be hungry just coming out of school. The mum inside her still existed.

The situation calmed, and Mum apologised. She bravely asked if she could meet Liezel Ann's mum. The day ended well, although everyone was traumatised.

A few days later, she went to see Liezel Ann's mum. Mama Elizabeth was gracious, calm and equally brave to meet with her, my Eder and my sister-in-law.

Liezel's mum explained everything that happened between her and Dad. By this time, Mum was a bit sober. Knowing her husband of 50 years, she believed every word that Mama Elizabeth said. She knew Dad was to blame for all this indiscretion. All of them were victims – Liezel Ann, Mama Elizabeth, my brother, my sister-in-law, their children and especially Mum.

Mum could not get herself to go back to San Francisco and see Dad. She was still very hurt. Instead, she came to Sydney, and I asked her to stay with me for as long as she liked. She can even stay with me forever, if that suits her. Knowing Mum and how independent she was, she would never stay with someone else – even if it's her child's house. She would always say, 'Never be a burden to anyone.' She never wanted to be a burden to anyone. She would say later in life, 'I want to be alone.'

She enjoyed her stay with me as much as I did. It was an opportunity for her to tell me her stories, her version – stories I never heard before. It was a beautiful mother-daughter bonding for a few weeks.

When the time of going home arrived, she said, 'That's it. I'm going back to San Francisco. I'm ready to face Dad again.'

Although I knew she wasn't ready to go home and face Dad, I could see that she missed him so much. She had so many reasons to miss him. Dad was such a charming man. He was always the life of the party. He was a fascinating storyteller. He had life adventures told in technicolour in the days of black and white conversations. He had an energy that filled rooms with joy and excitement. He played the piano without proper know-how and training, knowing only the key of C, but confidently played like he was a master concert pianist. He would sing stupid, silly songs, and everyone would sing and go along with his lead. He was everyone's favourite brother, cousin, uncle, friend, neighbour. He was Grandma's favourite son. He was full of great optimism and positive vibes. He believed he had everything even if he had, in fact, nothing much. He was such a character, really larger than life.

Mum went home to San Francisco still with a heavy heart but ready to move on. An opportunity came when Eric had a conference in Florida a few months later. I decided, my boys and I were going to tag along and visit Disney World. I organised for us to visit Mum in San Francisco before we headed to Eric's conference in Florida.

When in San Francisco, I dreaded seeing my dad. One year was not enough to heal the pain. I still had so much anger in my heart. We stayed in a hotel instead of staying at Mum and Dad's house. Mum was more nervous about us coming to see Dad than about dealing with her own pain. She had warned Dad that I was very upset and he had to be ready with whatever he would hear from me or whatever I would do.

When I asked Mum how she was, she said she was getting better and that Dad had been in his best behaviour since she arrived. He had been making her coffee, cooking breakfast, lunch and dinner for her, going to church with her every day, driving her around wherever she needed to be. He had been a very good husband to her. Even if she would argue with him concerning any matter (even the smallest of matters) and raise her voice, Dad would quietly listen and never say anything back to her. When she would finish her talk, he would just walk away like a meek lamb. Dad was so remorseful and had a contrite heart.

We invited them to have breakfast with us at the hotel. Mum walked towards me, and I quickly hugged her.

'Please go easy on Dad. I know you're still upset,' she whispered.

I almost cried hearing her words. How can Mum be so forgiving? If she was moving on, so should I. I decided I would just observe and let my emotions out of the way.

Dad looked at me without saying anything, then handed me a handwritten letter. He loved to write letters. I supposed it was an apology letter, so I took it and kept it in my bag for later reading. Eric and the boys have now arrived at the breakfast lounge, and everything went normally. The boys gave their grandma and grandpa their *mano po*, a Filipino gesture for respect, and their biggest hugs. It was such a lovely moment.

Apologies

Men are not very good at apologies, including Dad. After our breakfast and Mum and Dad had left, I read Dad's letter to me. He said that the news of him having a love child seemed to hit our family like an earthquake with a Richter scale of 7.3 magnitude. He was referring to the Ruby Tower Earthquake because it was a trauma we will always remember, and he felt bad that he wasn't there to be with us, especially since the next day was my birthday.

As I read the letter, I realised that it was not an apology letter. It was a letter to justify why he did what he did. He said he didn't say anything since the news broke because he knew that everything would cool down naturally in time. I hated that it wasn't an apology but a narrative of his circumstances.

I was no longer going to dwell in this. There was no point. As long as Mum was moving on, I'd have to accept that it had all happened in the past. We cannot undo it. I just had to accept things the way they were.

Meeting Liezel Ann

Although things seemed to have settled in San Francisco and I said I was going to move on from this dark past, it was not enough for me. There was still something missing.

I needed to heal.

In 2005, I went back to Manila and stayed in the penthouse apartment of my wonderful friend, Isabel. I told her the whole story and that I needed closure with my dad's indiscretion. She provided me with space and encouraged me to meet my dad's daughter.

Eder arranged for me to meet Liezel Ann after school, which was close to the penthouse. I was so nervous meeting her for the first time, so Isabel came with me.

'Liezel Ann?' I approached the 16-year-old innocent, young lady standing at the bus stop.

She shyly nodded her head.

She's so beautiful and pure. She looked angelic. She exuded a very respectful and unassuming demeanour, and I could feel the calmness of Dad, which she must have inherited from him. This young girl had Eder's features. I can't deny she's one of us. She's my baby sister. This poor kid was a victim of my dad's poor judgment.

Overwhelmed with mixed sentiments, still having unresolved heartaches with Dad, and anxious about meeting her, I suddenly felt a whole electric current run through from my brain, spine, arms, body, legs – my whole being. I felt limp with emotions.

I loved her so much already. It was unconditional love. How could she have grown up like this even without a dad? Who raised her? To what extent was she abandoned by Dad? How was she harassed by Mum? Was she taken care of properly? There were so many more questions than answers. I could not believe what just happened. I gave her a big hug, and we both cried.

Isabel invited her over for dinner. She was also welcomed to spend the night at the penthouse so we could talk and bond more. It was the beginning of a beautiful sister-to-sister relationship.

Catholic pilgrimage in Europe

In 2008, my mum turned 75. Despite five years passing since finding the birth certificate, there was still leftover hurt and pain. Over and over again, my mum would tell stories of how she would just snap at Dad, almost at anything minor, to bring up that he betrayed her. It seemed that we would never really get over this dark family episode. Mum was still hurting.

I decided I was going to do something good for Mum to help her heal. We would all gather in San Francisco with my siblings and our children from Texas, California and Manila, together with our relatives and friends, and celebrate Mum's major milestone. We would have a big event.

Remembering one of our conversations when she visited me in Sydney, she said, 'I thought I'd finished all my hardships at 70 years old. I thought I'd been through it all. Yet, here's another one. I thought, in our later years, Dad and I would just be travelling, enjoying life together. I've always envied our friends who shared their pictures of happy travels. Now this will never happen.'

Before the birthday celebration, I was going to give her a very special present. I asked Mum where she wanted to travel. As a devout Catholic, she said, 'I wish I could see the grotto of Our Lady of Lourdes.'

I knew this was also one of Dad's dreams – to be able to travel to holy places. As I was still quite upset with him for his ultimate betrayal of mum and the lame letter, I wanted to get even with him. I wanted to hurt him as much as he has hurt Mum. He was always hurt by exclusion, so I would take Mum to a catholic pilgrimage without Dad. He would be very envious and hurt.

Aldrina and I organised a catholic pilgrimage to Europe, highlighting a few days in Lourdes, France. Mum was very happy. It was indeed our ultimate revenge on Dad. We were going to have a great trip without him.

From San Francisco, we joined a catholic tour organised from Chicago. It was our first time doing something like this, and all of us were excited. We met a lot of people and went to a lot of religious places. It was a trip of a lifetime for us.

Mum was happy, yet something was missing. Throughout our tour, she kept saying, 'Wow, this is amazing. Dad would have loved this. I wish he were here.' Every new experience, every new site, every taste of new food, every new church we visit, she would say, 'Dad would have loved this. Wish he were here.'

Meanwhile, Aldrina's phone kept ringing. It was Dad.

'Did your mum drink her medication? At 12.00, make sure you apply the eyedrops in her left eye, then again in her right eye at 1 pm. How's your mum? Is she enjoying the trip? Make sure she doesn't get tired, ok? Did she eat enough breakfast? Are you looking after her very well? You know, when she's frustrated, she can easily snap. You should be patient with her, ok? Do not disrespect her. Just do as she says.'

Aldrina would tell Mum that Dad is calling. 'Mum, it's Dad. Would you like to speak to him?'

'Aghhh! No! Why would I want to speak to him? I don't care. Why is he calling, anyway? I don't want to hear his voice,' Mum would say.

Aldrina and I would quietly chuckle, knowing that there was a secret code of love between these two. Like young lovers having a silly quarrel, they still have so much love in their hearts for each other.

Throughout our trip, this scenario kept happening.

One day in Lourdes, we went to the baths, where miracles happen. We went on a very long queue early in the morning to experience the Holy Baths. We were instructed not to bring anything – no towels, no spare clothing. We didn't know what to expect.

When it was our turn to get in the baths, we were asked to take off all our clothes and put on a white robe provided by the nuns. There were at least five cubicles with curtains to the baths. In each bath, there were a couple of nuns to take care of the pilgrim. We all went to separate curtained cubicles almost at the same time.

Once inside, we stepped in the tub, and the nuns took off our robes. At the end of the tub was a statue of Our Lady of Lourdes. The nuns had a white blanket wrapped around us. They dipped the blanket, and in we went deep down the tub of miracle water – not holy water, but miracle water. That's what they called it. We were to say a prayer of intercession to the Lady and kiss the statue.

Everything was a blur. I was dragged through the tub by the blanket, and a blinding light overcame me. As if I was embraced by the Immaculate Mother, I was taken out of this world and a powerful, peaceful energy ran through my being. It was electrifying. It felt like forever and as if I was knocked out of consciousness. For a single moment in time, it was as if time and space froze, and everything was ok. It was an experience beyond words.

I suddenly felt the tap of one of the nuns, saying, 'You can head over to put your clothes back on.'

It's over. It's done. Time at the bath was done.

Half-conscious and half-asleep, I knew I was no longer in a trance. I quietly put on my clothes. Even without a towel, my whole body was miraculously dry! I just walked out the curtain through the exit area, but like an earthquake with an aftershock, I wasn't over with this spiritual experience. I found myself crying. I didn't know why I was crying or if this was tears of joy or sorrow or repentance or forgiveness. I cried and cried and cried. I just needed to cry. I had to let it out, and it felt good.

In one corner, there were two ladies hugging each other, also crying – my mum and my sister. We all hugged one another and asked ourselves, 'What was that experience? Why are we crying?'

We could not answer our own questions, and we all started to laugh as we felt a little bit overly dramatic and crazy. We composed ourselves as if nothing had happened. We all walked out of the baths, smiling on a high, as if we weren't crying moments earlier. It was a sacred calm. It was forgiveness. And we all knew it was glorious.

It was such a special moment shared with so much peace in our hearts.

As we returned to San Francisco, Dad was at the airport to pick us up. We all gave him our *mano po* and biggest hugs. The narrative of the baths was: 'We were dunked in a tub of water at the baths. The miracle was that we were dry and didn't even need a towel when we changed back to our clothing. It was amazing!'

Dad was so happy to hear our stories. Everything was back to normal. The dark past has been overshadowed by the glow of the holy experience at the baths. *Forgiveness* was the word of the day.

He welcomed us with our favourite dish and his signature cooking, Grandpa's steak. Unforgettable celebrations for Mum's 75th birthday followed after a few days.

---

*Lesson 8: Forgiveness is a
powerful act that fosters peace.*

December 1968 – Christmas in Saigon, Vietnam, visiting my dad during the height of the Vietnam War. This was a Polaroid photo, warped on the edges, saved during our house fire in 1980.

Two nuns of EDSA – An iconic photo of the EDSA peaceful people power revolution in 1986. Two daughters of St Paul are leading the prayers bravely fronting the battle tank. My brother, wearing white shirt and dark shades behind the nuns, was included in the photo. I was somewhere in the crowds. Mum was so proud of us being part of this historic event.

Photo credit to Manila Times photo artist Pete Reyes. Photo taken in 24 February 1986.

The light gate was our humble apartment and doubled up as our business address when we turned it into a software house from December 1988 to October 1991. This picture was taken when we visited in 2016, reminding us of our humble beginnings.

DEAR TATTA:

MANY, MANY HAPPY RETURNS
OF THE DAY. SO SORRY THIS
WAS DELAYED. WERE ALL OCCUPIED
AND NEARLY OVERLOOK ABOUT THIS
DAY; BUT SURELY, IT IS AN IMPORTANT
DAY FOR US & FOR YOU.

GOT YOUR LETTER; HAVE NOT TIME
YET TO ANSWER IN DETAILS. WERE
STILL PRAYING DAILY ROSARY FOR
YOUR AUSSIE PROJECT. DON'T WORRY,
KEEP COOL AS THIS WAITING, AN
AGONIZING WAITING FOR THE "D DAY"
IS NOTHING BUT A TEST OF TIME /
DESTINY PROGRAMMED "UPSTAIR".
PLS HAVE PATIENCE, IT WILL BE
THROUGH IN DUE TIME.
WERE ALL OK.
WE LOVE YOU ALL.

DAD & MOM

This was Dad's birthday greetings in August 1991 at the back of a beautiful birthday card. I was lost and didn't know what my next steps would be after my redundancy and after we closed our little software house. Prayer was our strength, and faith was our teacher in patience. Dad knew and believed in God's perfect timing. He called it 'Upstairs programming'.

November 1991, when we first arrived in Australia. My wonderful aunt took us to Waratah Park to enjoy the kangaroos and other Aussie animals.

Raising our boys in Catholic faith. This was our eldest son's first communion day at St Mary's church in Rydalmere in 1994.

Photo taken in November 2008, with my sister and Mum when we experienced forgiveness, peace and gratitude at the Baths in Lourdes, France. It was the 150th anniversary of the apparition of the Virgin Mary at The Grotto of Massabielle, Shrine of Lourdes.

Celebrating Mum's 75th birthday in San Francisco, CA, where all kinds of miracles blessed our lives. This was our family photo with Mum, Dad, Marylou, Bert, Aldrina and Eder.

In 2009, celebrating our 25th wedding anniversary with a grand renewal of vows in Sydney. One of the many events we hosted to create an inclusive environment for all family members. My brother and his family travelled from Manila. Mum, Dad, my sister and her family travelled from California for this most memorable and happiest of times. In this photo, Eric's entire family and my beautiful aunt (in front, wearing white top) and uncle who supported us and continues to be our inspiration and role model.

After Dad passed away in April 2012, he made his presence known in rainbows and roses. In September 2016, the day after Liz and Jay's wedding, we travelled to Lopez, Quezon to visit Dad's tomb as a sign of love and respect. We had so much fun along the way on this five-hour drive, sharing stories, exchanging jokes and endless laughter. We called it a group honeymoon, as we chaperoned our newlyweds on this journey. We had a short break at Daph's Café. We walked along the beach to take photos. To our surprise, there was a perfect rainbow behind us! This was our photo of my brother, sisters, nephew and our spouses. Thank you, Dad, for your presence.

My near-drowning trauma has turned into my favourite time of the week when I enjoy this healthy exercise. I swim 1,200 metres at the local pool.

Travellling to tick off our bucket list in our retirement years. Dreams do come true. This is our perfect trifecta, balancing health, time and money. A trip to South America, visiting Chile, Brazil, Argentina, Ecuador and Peru. The sacred citadel of Macchu Picchu was one of the highlights of our wonderful vacation.

Building great relationships and strong bonds are some of my wealth secrets. Over 40 years of friendship, we all met at work in Rorer-Philippines. Up to today, we continue to enjoy this deep connection. We know our families well. We keep in touch almost daily. We go on holidays together and always have a good laugh. We pray together. We inspire one another. We share good, helpful information with one another. We share our personal ebbs and tides and celebrate our success. The man in the middle was our mentor in life and in financial literacy.

Thank you
DEAR : KORA
THANK YOU FOR
ALL YOUR HELP!

Thank You
Thank You Cora
for all your help I will
never be able to thank you
enough.
Lots of love

Hi Cora,

Thank you so much for all your support & kindness during the hardest time of my life.

You're the angel God sent me during this tuff time and I'm so grateful to know you.

You're in my prayers, God bless you.

Yours sincerly

Good Morning Cora,
I'm so overwhelmed with being a mother to 4 children one being a new born on my own.
Apologies for taking a few days to get this to you but it's hard to find time .

Here is my electricity bill also would you be able to speak with some one in the commonwealth bank. I'm so behind on this account I don't know what to do anymore my soul is truly broken.

You have been a god sent & I don't know what I would do if I hadn't had your help in this time of terrible heartache ... Thank You SO MUCH Cora

Yay!!!!! Oh my goodness thank you THANK YOU THANK YOU SOOOOO MUCH Cora!!!
I am so super excited right now, I cannot tell you how happy I feel knowing that that weight of debt is off my shoulders!
I agree to everything below...with a big smile too!
Thank you so much!

Kind Regards

What do I collect? Thank-you cards, thank-you notes, thank-you emails, thank-you hugs, thank-you drawings from little children. Here are some of them in recent days. It warms my heart to know that I have lifted a weight off someone's emotional burden and that they are grateful. Gratitude is the key that opens abundance.

9

Family dynamics –
Our gems and jewels

A gem cannot be polished without friction
nor a person perfected without challenge.
– Lucius Annaeus Seneca

Raising our family

We were making small, consistent progress in Sydney. From a mould-infested unit in Fairfield, we moved to a three-bedroom house in Ryde, close to work. The story Eric will not forget is a conversation he had with the removalist, asking him, 'How long did you stay in this unit?'

Eric replied, 'Eight months. We had to complete the lease contract agreement.'

'Wow! Eight months! Really?' The removalist replied. 'I wouldn't last a day here. How did you put up with all the moulds?'

Eric wouldn't say anything back but thought, *How dare he say that? He looks so untidy and unkempt, like mould lives in him.*

But it was funny. One day in 1992, when my mum visited from San Francisco, she wouldn't even sleep in our unit. She stayed with Aunty. When she first entered our apartment, she said, 'Do you have an air freshener?' Not that we didn't keep the unit clean, fresh and tidy. It was just a miserable, cheap, stinky place.

When at Ryde, the removalist unloaded our furniture we obtained from Salvos, he quipped, 'Wow, this is a better place. Definitely better.'

It was a big house. Although old, it had a lot of space where we could invite family and friends. In February 1993, my dad's brother visited us from Manila. We hosted his birthday, which we cherish so much, realising later that it would be his last birthday. It was so special.

In this house, we were also able to host Eric's mum, dad, sister and uncle during their few weeks' holiday in Sydney. As well, we hosted a few new migrant friends to sleep over on some weekends.

Unfortunately, we did not stay long in this house. One day, we came home and, like an earthquake of yet another kind, our house was broken into and ransacked – money, jewellery, and things were stolen. Everything was everywhere – clothes out of the drawers, furniture overturned, picture frames broken, paperwork strewn everywhere. We felt so violated. Our privacy was invaded. It was a traumatising experience for us because we thought Sydney was a very safe place compared to where we came from. We never expected this to happen to us.

We were fortunate to quickly be able to move to a townhouse just across the public school in Dundas. It was a lovely complex with good neighbours. The kids went to the school across the road. They would just press the pedestrian push button to go to school.

It reminded me of when we lived in Orosa Street, just across St Paul College.

One thing I learned from Mum was to live close to school. It allowed the kids to sleep in a few extra minutes every day, which is vital to their health, growth and wellbeing.

As the boys were growing up, I changed jobs to make sure I worked within the 5-kilometre radius of home. My children were my priority. I wanted to be there to help them with their homework and make dinner for them at night. If anything happened at school, I wanted to be there quickly. I made sure I did what my mum wasn't able to do for me. I wanted my children to have better childhood experiences compared to what I had growing up.

Even with my fulltime work, I made sure I volunteered on most committees at school to support my children – canteen duties, sports duties on weekends, setting up grounds, BBQ duty, scoring at baseball games, school fete stall duties, Mother's Day stall duties, Education Day, sports carnivals, Easter hat parades, Christmas carols, among many more. One day, I volunteered at school to teach my son's classmates about Philippine history and culture. Most importantly, we didn't miss a single parent-teacher meeting.

Each time I did something for my children, I felt like I was doing it for myself, wishing I had my mum present in my childhood days at school. One day, during the Education Day picnic with parents, I was with my son having lunch at school. He was so proud that I, his mum, was there with him. We shared his favourite meal, adobo, a Filipino dish, with some of the boys at school. I remembered how my classmates had shared their food with me at the Las Brisas excursion when I was 10 years old. One boy said, 'Can you teach my mum how to make this dish? It's yummy.'

That night, one of my neighbours, whose son also attended the same school, just straight from her work, called me and said, 'My son is so upset with me. He said he was the only boy in the whole school without a mum during Education Day picnic lunch. Is that true? Did you go there? He said that they were all eating adobo, and he was having his usual Nutella sandwich alone without a mum.'

While it was a struggle to raise a family with fulltime work, manage the household, maintain good relationships, engage in further studies and make time for exercise, this was the best and most cherished part of our family life. It seemed tough and exhausting while we were going through it – the late nights and the early mornings, the running around to drive the kids to their games and practices and birthday parties and events. But looking at it now, they were gifts of an abundant life. The weekend baseball games; the karate classes; the tennis tournaments; the Yu-Gi-Oh conventions; the Pokemon competitions; the high school musicals; the trip to the Opera House for the recorder performance; the first communions; the sacraments of confirmation and reconciliation; our holidays to the snows, to Disneyland, to Gold Coast, to Port Macquarie, to Melbourne, to San Francisco, to LA, to Florida, to Seattle, to Canada, to Manila, and so many more to mention – these were all the blessings we were grateful for. These are our precious gems and jewels – a wealth of experience no home invader can steal or take away from us.

Sharing what we have

The next step towards migration is sharing our newfound life of opportunities with those we love. My husband's family in Manila were first on our list. We started inviting my in-laws for a holiday in Sydney. From 1993, Sydney became the second home of my in-laws. They would spend weeks and months with us, enjoying time with our growing boys. We would go away on trips around Sydney and New South Wales.

Eric's brother, Ryan, and his wife organised their honeymoon in Sydney and used our guest room as their honeymoon suite. Years later, they returned to take their first overseas family trip in Sydney together with their baby daughter.

His other brother, Adam, and his wife also had their honeymoon in our guest suite. While another brother, Louis, used his trip pass as a pilot to occasionally visit on some long weekends and some planned extended holidays. His sister, Pam, also came to visit with his mum, dad and favourite uncle. Our home welcomed my family too – my mum and dad, Marylou and her daughter and husband, my other sister, Mae, and her two boys, my uncles, aunties, cousins, friends.

Our home eventually turned into a happy Airbnb, mainly for my in-laws. We became tourist guides, event organisers and house managers for our family guests. Eventually, Eric invited and sponsored each of his brothers and their families to migrate to Australia.

One by one, his brothers started arriving as permanent residents. We opened our homes and welcomed them to the lucky country, a wonderful reality some Filipinos can only dream about. This was us paying forward for my uncle and aunt giving us a warm welcome when we first arrived. It was great. My mum and dad were so proud of us. From not finding work to settling down, to being able to accommodate and host families and friends for months, and now being able to change lives through sponsorship and support.

Adam, his wife and his son were the first to arrive. Eric has the biggest heart. Once they arrived, he settled them quickly. He didn't want Adam to experience any of his frustrating and depressing days of endlessly looking for work or working in the jelly factory or volunteering for free to get a local experience. Before Adam arrived, Eric had organised a role for him at Microsoft through his internal networking. On day one, Adam had work waiting for him.

Eric was always very supportive of him. After Adam had finished his university degree in computer engineering, Eric immediately offered him a role in our little software house so he could get work experience in software programming. Even in choosing his university course, Eric was the one who encouraged him to take a computer engineering degree. He had the foresight that this was the career of the future. Eric, being the eldest son, similar to my dad, always kept his role as the big brother and was always there for his younger siblings, most especially to Adam.

When they first visited Sydney on their honeymoon, it was also Eric who encouraged them to apply for a permanent resident visa. He pledged full support for them. Once they arrived, we provided everything for them – transport, accommodation, meals, board, childminding, the lot. It reminded us of how my aunt and uncle treated us. Eric wanted to make sure Adam and his family had nothing to worry about. He just wanted them to focus on settling in with their new environment and integrating well into the Australian culture. Because they both worked at the same office in Microsoft, he provided transport every day for many years, not charging him a single cent of petrol or any form of contribution. It reminded me of my wonderful cousin who did the same for me for one year, when we both worked in St Leonards.

Adam's son shares a birthday with Eric. On this day, Eric would always organise a family-and-friends get together to celebrate more of his nephew's birthday rather than his. This was Eric's way of sharing his joy with Adam and his family. It was immense.

I wish I had a brother who would support me the way Adam was supported.

Louis was next to arrive. He was single and held a pilot's license in the Philippines. It was no longer his intention to pursue his career as a pilot once he arrived in Australia. He applied for a student visa to gain a degree in Transport. When he arrived, I organised a role at Pfizer for him to be my temp assistant, even if he didn't have any office work experience. We never wanted anyone to go through our difficult and dark days of finding work. We wanted to make it easy and smooth for all of them. It was great.

It was supposed to be a temporary arrangement to give him work experience and some income while on a student visa. The temporary arrangement turned into a pathway for a new career for him. It was incredible! Louis pursued a career in accountancy, later becoming a CPA to continue working at Pfizer. He worked there for many years.

Ryan arrived with his wife and three young children. His intention was to continue being a pilot and leave his family here with us. The same form of support was given to them – assurance of support and bond money to Centrelink, sponsorship support, application for Medicare, Centrelink and Transport NSW. After a couple of weeks after arriving in Australia, Ryan left for Japan, where he would work as a pilot. He would visit his family every six weeks and stay with us for two weeks each time. When they arrived, Eric's mum came with them.

We looked after Ryan's wife, their three young children and Eric's mum. It was quite a challenge to have three small children in our house. By this time, our boys were already in high school, and we were no longer used to having small children actively running around the house.

We supported Ryan's wife in every way we could. It was difficult for her to look after the children on her own. She was used to having household help in Manila. It reminded me of our time when we were new migrants in my aunt's house. Her children would constantly look for their nannies and their dad, having difficulty adjusting to their new environment. They would uncontrollably play up sometimes. It was a challenging time for all. But following my aunt's example, we continued to be patient, kind, understanding and supportive. All things settled, and we helped them move out to their own house, where the children had their own space.

Years later, by the Balance of Family migration scheme, we were able to sponsor Eric's parents, eventually leaving just his sister, Pam in the Philippines. After years of eligibility, Pam was sponsored to join all of us under the Last Remaining Relative visa scheme. A couple of years later, her husband followed and joined her in Sydney.

Our home was always busy, accommodating families for months on end for many years. There were lots of good memories and some minor discords dealing with different personalities and challenging circumstances.

With our growing boys; a fulltime work; doing my master's degree; playing tourist guide, house manager, all-round driver and chef; managing our husband–wife relationship; relationship with my family, self-care and exercise, sometimes it was all too exhausting – like I was a vehicle always running on empty, or as my dad would say, 'Low *batt ka na,*' referring to a mobile phone with low battery battery charge.

I didn't know how we all got through, but Eric has the kindest heart. He would always say, 'This is our pay-forward. Aunty and Uncle were very kind and generous to us. We have to do the same.'

Everyone eventually settled in, moved to their own houses and lived independently. The years that followed saw us regularly organising events – birthdays, Christmas, Mother's Day, Father's Day, anniversaries and long weekends – so we could gather family together. So many times, we organised mahjong playdates with Eric's mum and dad or random lunch or dinner or weekends away.

In 2009, Eric and I celebrated our 25th wedding anniversary with everyone – both mums and dads, siblings, nephews, nieces, aunts, uncles, the lot. It was an amazing event that brought families and friends together. This anniversary celebration was my gift to my mum because she was very disappointed during our very simple wedding 25 years ago. I couldn't even wear a long gown and she couldn't even invite her friends. Finally, she was happy.

In 2010, we celebrated Eric's parents' 50th wedding anniversary. We celebrated major milestones – 18th, 21st, 30th, 40th, 50th and 60th birthdays of family members, Christmases, the works. This is what families do. This is what is important. This is our wealth, our gems, our jewels.

Whereas before, we used to send photos and say, *'Wish you were here',* lonely without family, now we are all here. We are complete. We are very happy. I'm so proud of Eric for doing all this for his family. There aren't a lot of families in Australia that are complete, enjoying time together. I envied them. For my family to be together, we needed to organise it well in advance. My mum, dad and siblings were all over the world – Manila, California, Texas, Sydney. Because of the huge effort of Eric his family are all here, and it is very special. If they want to gather together as a family, they can.

Years pass, and things change. People change. Circumstances change. Unfortunately, for many years now, we have been actively excluded from family events especially organised by Adam and his wife. Adam, his wife and his son do not even know my phone number of 30 years. They don't communicate. There's no 'Merry Christmas' or 'Happy Birthday' or 'How are you?'. There's no checking in. For some unknown reason, we were unfriended and blocked from social media. In an effort to always include family, an invite was sent to them for the special celebration of Eric's 60th birthday. An RSVP was received, confirmed that they were attending. Seats were paid for and reserved for them. Only to have them empty on the night. We did not hear a single word of apology or explanation of their non-attendance. It was extremely disappointing, considering that seats were limited during this period of COVID restrictions and we wanted to invite other friends but gave them the priority. What a shame.

Around Christmas, when Eric's dad passed away, I sent Adam a text message and he replied, 'Who is this?' An ultimate demonstration of pitiful estrangement and ungratefulness.

Liezel Ann

After meeting Liezel Ann in 2005, we kept in touch a few times. Eder and Liz (as we now fondly call her) have developed a pure sisterly love relationship between them since that fateful day in 2005 at Chowking. Eder invited her to her home a few times, and her children have grown very close to their new aunt.

During one summer, Eder, who works in Cathay Pacific and is based in Hong Kong, invited her for a working holiday so Liz can spend time with her children. Eder organised all her paperwork, plane ticket, passport and all travel documents. Liz stated that she never thought she would ever have a passport in her life, let alone get on a plane and travel to Hong Kong. That trip opened her eyes and mind to what could be possible.

In 2012, Dad passed away. From Manila, she travelled to Lopez, Quezon to attend the funeral with her best friend, even with the stern warning from her mum not to attend because anything nasty might happen. She was so determined to see Dad for the last time, no matter what might happen.

Although she stayed in Mum and Dad's house together with all of us, we kept it a secret from Mum, letting her sleep in the basement bedroom, where Mum would never go. During the funeral viewing, she would go to the chapel only if Mum was not there. When Mum would go to the chapel, we would ask Liz to leave and go back to the house so that they would not meet. Our relatives were already asking, 'Who is this young girl?' but we would just ignore them.

On the day of the funeral, there was no more hiding. Everyone was present. Liz bravely faced Mum and presented her a mass card and very respectfully said, 'Condolences *po*.'

Mum, still so filled with mixed emotions, graciously said, 'Thank you for the mass card. Have you seen your Papa? If not, go and see him and say goodbye. This is your last chance to do so.'

Although stunned, some shocked, by the revelation of Dad's love child, everyone demonstrated grace, maturity and love when we introduced Liz to all the uncles and aunts and cousins and everyone at the funeral. It was such a delight that she was warmly welcomed and accepted by the whole family, carefully being respectful to my mum. This was how Dad would have wanted it to be. One uncle was so happy to meet her because they found out that they share the same birthday. He said, 'From now on, I can be your papa. You can call me Papa if you want.'

Liz said that her life had changed since the funeral, and all that she was seeking for, she seemed to have found some answers. The next years saw her completing her university degree in nursing and travelling to Singapore to seek greener pastures.

In 2016, Liz got married, and we travelled to the Philippines to attend as godparents. Eric got the biggest role of his life when he got to walk Liz to the altar. My brother, who was supposed to do the role, was late for the procession, having been caught in traffic.

Eric was so happy, extremely proud that he had walked the aisle with his pseudo-daughter on her wedding day. After all, Liz was only one month younger than our miracle baby. She absolutely qualifies to be the daughter we never had. Walking the bride to the altar was an experience privileged to a few, which not everyone can have, nor was it an experience that will ever be repeated for him. What makes it more special is that it was an unexpected experience. It was pure gold!

I was the biggest drama queen on her wedding day. She asked me at the last minute if I could do a speech, and I said yes. I was so nervous, as I don't usually do speeches, let alone an impromptu speech. All I could think of was all the years we missed out on building a relationship with her because we didn't know she existed. I felt responsible for making up for all of Dad's misgivings and shortcomings. I promised in front of all their guests that I would never allow that to happen again. I will take care of Liz as Dad would have wanted us to.

I couldn't control my emotions that I have kept in me for so long, like my mum's time when she found out about Dad's indiscretion and went to Uncle Manny. I cried a river. I cried and cried so hard that I probably touched people's hearts; everyone started crying. It felt like there was no dry eye in the reception hall.

It was embarrassing. I wanted to disappear. At the end of the speech, there was a standing ovation, and everyone wanted to hug me. I wanted to hug everyone back. It was such an incredible event that ended in so much love and commitment, not only between the newly married couple but also between long-lost sisters.

After the wedding, Liz and her husband expressed interest in applying for a permanent resident visa in Australia. I was so excited that I could finally have a sister with me in Sydney. Every now and again, my cousins and circle of close friends would go out for a girls' day out, and I was the only one without a sister. Finally, I can say that I am with my sister on our next girls' day out.

Liz and her husband worked their way into getting their permanent resident visas approved without any help from us. They arrived in June 2018. The only thing we did was pick them up from the airport – such a big contrast from what we did to support Eric's family. It was a happy event to welcome them. We organised my aunts, uncles, cousins, friends and Eric's family to join us. It was a happy occasion, but unfortunately, unbeknownst to us, that would be their last meeting with Uncle, as he would pass away three months after the welcome party.

Having them at home was some of the best days of our lives. It was such a pleasure to share dinner and catch up on life. We shared similar experiences of migrating to another country – theirs was Singapore, ours was Australia. There were endless stories to tell;

we never ran out of topics to talk about. We learned so much from one another. Her husband is also an engineer and went to the same university as Eric.

Our home was so blessed with so much love and laughter when they stayed with us. Liz had the energy of our dad that she brought to our home, radiating with good vibes and all things positive. Although we didn't grow up together, I felt that Liz grew up with me. We shared the same values, laughed at the same jokes, enjoyed the same food and watched the same TV shows. Our boys loved their new cousin (Liz's daughter) so much. They also learned a lot from their Aunt Liz, whom they treated as an elder, although she was younger than them. She was a godsend. She is definitely the daughter I never had and, at the same time, the sister that I can share my dad's teachings with.

In a few weeks, they moved out and found their own rented accommodation. I wish they hadn't left yet, as we were really enjoying time with them, especially with their daughter, who was such a delight to have at home. Mum always said to me, 'Do not be a burden. Do not overextend your stay in your aunty's house.' It was as if Liz knew and heard what my mum would say if they stayed for a few more weeks.

There's this sacred bond between us, as if she were also raised by my mum and dad and knew the 10 Commandments of Human Relations. They were never a burden to us. They were always helpful around the house – doing chores, cleaning, cooking and helping with shopping, even if I asked them not to bother. They were so much like my dad, who would always think and say, 'Make sure you carry your own weight in every situation. Always add value.'

After they left, we became so much closer to each other. We spend alternate Christmas and other events between our homes. They are always in touch with us. Despite her busy schedule juggling mum duties, fulltime work, managing her household and supporting her mum, she always finds the time to call or send messages on how their week went and just check in on us if we are ok.

Family dynamics

Eric and I are a perfect match. He has four brothers and one sister, while I have four sisters and one brother. Amazing! During our wedding, we paired them all together to do the readings, candles, veil and arras. Simple. Done!

The dynamics of brotherhood and sisterhood are so much different. Growing up in a family of girls, my sisterhood experience was one of being cooperative, collaborative, supportive, emotionally present and compassionate. Growing up in his family of boys, I noticed the brotherhood experience was more of being competitive, transactional, straightforward and solution-seeking. With the exception of their sister Pam, who has the heart of a true sister, I would never understand their concept of siblinghood.

Family dynamics are an interesting thing. Every family has some sort of unique dynamic, oftentimes complex and fascinating than we realise.

For many years, Eric worked so hard towards bringing all his family together creating an inclusive envronment. Within our circle of friends, his efforts are admired by many in supporting his whole family to migrate to Australia., We hear how they have profound gratitude to their relative who has pioneered their family migration that is why they have profound regard and respect for us.

The case of Eric was even more special. He not only encouraged, sponsored and supported his family through their residency journey, but he also had practical measures to ensure that they would not go through the difficulties we had. His support extended to help them have work waiting for them. He set them up to succeed. For many years, he continued to support them in looking after their wives and children, especially during emergencies.

I remember getting in trouble with my manager at work when I failed to show up on a day I had a very important deadline to meet. The night before, Ryan's son had a medical emergency. I stayed in the hospital with Ryan's wife. Ryan was in Japan, and Eric and his brothers were all out of town for work. Eric asked our sons to go to Ryan's house to take care of their young cousins during the night in the absence of their parents. The next day, Ryan's wife stayed in the hospital with their sick son, and as our sons had to go to school, I had to rush to their house to take care of their girls in the morning and get organised for school and daycare and then afternoon pick up. My boss was outraged that I didn't turn up for work that day. Later on, he would use this incident to cite as one of the reasons why I had to be redundant at work. This is a story we will remember but is not in their place of history that will ever be talked about or acknowledged.

Similar to the support we received from my aunt and uncle, we sincerely paid it forward by helping everyone settle down the best we can. Except for Pam, who stayed with her parents as a new migrant, we welcomed all of them to our home and provided temporary accommodation and meals; helped with child minding; introduced them to our circle of good friends; gave them work opportunities; took them out for weekend getaways; drove them around to shops, church and school; gave driving lessons; helped to purchase their cars; enrolled the children to school; assisted in moving houses; bought furniture; communicated or checked in regularly and celebrated our wins together. This is what families do, as I am familiar with and as how we were raised by Mum and Dad. This is how family bonds and good relationships are built. This worked well with my aunt and me as we continue to build strong bonds and enjoy great relationships. Despite the minimal support Liz and Pam received from us, this worked well with them, too. And we continue to enjoy warm, affectionate, respectful and loving sisterhood.

When you are deliberately excluded in an inclusive environment you created, you send a text message to family you have invested so much love and heart into building great relationships, and you receive a cold reply of 'Who is this?', you wonder, *What kind of human deviation is this?* I used to ponder why and how this kind of human behaviour is developed. Out of curiosity, I asked them a direct question but did not obtain any answers. Pam, in her effort to resolve the elephant in the room, asked the same question. It was just flat out ignored.

I realised that I do not share the same values with them as I do with my aunt, Pam and Liz.

Lesson 9: The bond that links your true family is not one of blood but of respect and joy in each other's life.
– Richard Bach

10

Investing and wealthy living

Compound interest is the eighth wonder of the world.
– Albert Einstein

Creating and growing wealth

By the grace of God, we were able to save enough deposit to buy a house in 1996. We prioritised paying off our mortgage to save on interest. In 2001, we purchased another property to cater to the growing needs of our family, as we were constantly hosting as if running a hotel for weeks and months on end. This was an upgrade from our three-bedroom duplex to a six-bedroom home. We transferred our home loan to the new property and leased the duplex. As everyone was investing in property, we wanted to experience firsthand how it is to manage a rental property.

After 12 months and plenty of research, we decided property investment was not for us. We sold the duplex for almost twice the price of the original value in 1996. We put the proceeds of the sale into our new home mortgage, creating a huge issue with the bank. In seven years, we had fully paid our mortgage for both the duplex and the new house!

We received a letter from the bank, saying that we couldn't exit early from our home mortgage because the contract is 25 years to pay. There would be heavy penalties for paying it off early. Instead of exiting our loan, we thought of an idea that later worked to our advantage.

While lots of our friends advised that we should invest in property with the 100% equity we have, we did something else. We withdrew a small amount of 16% of our equity from the home loan account so we could maintain the loan for years, as per the contract. This way, we will not be penalised for early exit. We were going to pay the home loan interest at 7%, and we are looking at investing in long-term shares with growth of 9% to 15%. The 2% to 8% gap would be our margin and the beginning of our road to financial independence. Brilliant! Years later, this strategy would be called **debt recycling**.

We started our investment journey in 2004. Eric and I did our own research on budgeting, money management and wealth creation. We used to watch TV shows discussing money and wealth. He joined groups discussing investment options, and we listened to known and credible financial gurus trusted in the finance industry. We looked at growing our superannuation for a non-concessional contribution. Finally, we made the decision to invest our 16% (just a random number) home equity safely in low-cost index funds. The main consideration for this was the low-cost fees of managing the long-term investment.

In 2004, social media was still limited, and there were no learning videos yet from YouTube or TikTok. Today, it is so much easier to access information on investing and wealth creation.

The real secret to investing is time and consistency. Time is your friend. Consistency is your commitment to your goal. We were not experts in the field of investing, but through our years of experience, we have learned so much about investing. Like anything new and outside of our comfort zone, it was quite daunting to begin this process. We were cautious in choosing a reputable index fund. Like us and in life, our strategy was simple: Aim for a budget surplus, consistently top up our investments, set and forget. Reinvest the dividends. And no lifestyle creep.

After at least 20 years, we're ready to retire!

Building relationships – Living wealthy beyond the bank account

Wealth is beyond financial aspects that encompass various areas for living a life of abundance. Investing is not limited to property, liquid or digital assets. We also invest in relationships. It is imperative to build healthy relationships with family and friends. My dad had displayed a framed 'Ten Commandments of Human Relations' on our wall. Because we saw it every day, we had memorised it in our brains.

Dad was so big on human relations. We inherited that from him. We have great friends from university, high school and even kindergarten! We keep in touch with family members who are cousins twice or thrice removed. We keep the newfound friends we meet from our travels, our work, church, exercise groups and community. It is so wonderful to travel to cities and catch up with those we have these great relationships with.

Good relationships are worth every investment. However, not all investments in building a great relationship grow. No matter how much time, money, love and support you pour into it, good relationships only thrive when both sides are willing to nurture, grow and sustain the bond. Mum taught us the concept of reciprocity and balance. For a good relationship to flourish, give-and-take must exist. Communication has to be constant. There must be a genuine intention to build and make it strong. Some relationships, no matter how heavily you invest in them or how much time, commitment and love you put in, will fall on barren soil and never grow because you don't share the same values.

Like any investment, there are risks of losses along the way. Even in building relationships, we need to cut our losses, move along and invest our emotional bank in someone else. Toxic relationships and those that are not well-meaning should not be part of our portfolio.

Health and wellness

Big on our bucket list is investing in our health and wellness. Since our 20s, we have engaged in a healthy lifestyle. A healthy and nutritious diet is at the top of our list. Sleep is a priority over late-night outs. Exercise has been a part of our weekly routine. We have invested in gym memberships for at least 40 years, doing weight training, aerobic classes and mind-body-spirit group training exercises for physical health and mental wellbeing.

Many years ago, when raising our young children, Eric and I would wake up early in the morning to go to the gym together. That was our husband-wife bonding before it gets too busy for our many roles to fulfill during the day. It worked double purpose – to keep our bodies strong and also nurture our relationship during this stressful period of our lives, raising children and building our family and careers. Looking after our physical bodies and our mental health was essential.

Now in our 60s, we continue to be conscious of our health and be mindful of the exercise that our bodies allow. Eric continues to work out in the gym a few times a week. I have transitioned to the slower and more gentle exercises like walking, yoga, tai chi and body balance.

My memory of almost drowning in the swimming pool during our school excursion has turned into my favourite part of my week — I swim 1,200 metres for my weekly exercise. As a 10-year-old girl, I longed for proper swimming lessons. It was in my first year of university that I got those swimming lessons as a compulsory physical education subject.

Regular medical check-ups are now a part of our schedules. How can we enjoy life if our physical bodies are unwell? Part of ageing leads to physiological changes that affect bones, muscles, heart, eyesight, hearing, balance and brain functions. We need to be aware of our own physical conditions, monitor any chronic diseases, manage genetic and inherited conditions, and allow any early intervention to manage lifestyle changes as a result of ageing.

I am quite paranoid that dementia runs in our family, as my mum and all her siblings had it. With this awareness in mind, I do my part in preventing dementia, whether I develop it or not. I engage in fun games and activities that exercise the brain — mahjong is a pastime we enjoy as a family, I try to play the piano, I play online games and puzzles, and I write with my non-dominant hand. These are little exercises to help me.

Regardless of if and when I develop any disease in the future, I can honestly say to myself, I have done all I can to be healthy and strong. Outside of what I can control, I surrender, accept it graciously and embrace it as another human experience to complete my human puzzle.

It is sad when I hear stories of a sudden stroke or heart attack just because the individuals or their families are not aware that they have an existing medical condition, which otherwise could have been prevented if there had been early intervention. They may have neglected themselves by not having a regular health check. It is especially sad for those who are left half dead, left paralysed or in a coma for a long time. It is not only heartbreaking and costly; it puts a burden and pressure on caring family members to have parts of their lives dedicated to looking after them. I can almost hear my mum's words: 'Don't be a burden to anyone.'

I have had clients who save money all their lives, thinking of a happy retirement of leisure, travel or fulfilling lifelong passions and hobbies, only to spend it on medical expenses later in life. I have clients who just save money enough for their own decent funeral. That is not wealthy living. Invest in your health and wellness wisely. It is an essential aspect of financial independence.

Health is wealth.

Wealthy living

Mum said, 'If you were born poor, it's not your fault. But if you die poor, it is your responsibility.'

We have been taught personal responsibility since we were young children. Mum would never come to our rescue if we did something we got in trouble for that she had previously warned us about. We were always left to sort out the mess we had created.

'I told you so. What lesson did you learn from this? Now find a way to fix it,' Mum would say.

Growing up, I felt that Mum was so unsupportive and uncaring. Later, I realised that it was tough love, great resilience and creativity that she taught us. It's a gift. We never got in trouble as kids, as we would think of the consequences of our actions before doing something we might regret later on. In the rare cases that we got into some mess, as all kids do, we got very creative in finding solutions and responding positively.

I always think of this quote from my mum on being poor, dying poor and being responsible for our own poverty. I don't know where she got it from, but I took this seriously in my desire to get out of poverty.

I do not want to die poor. Since the opposite seems to be 'I want to die rich', all my life I focused on dying rich. I created a money mindset that I will not die poor; I will die rich.

Recently, I challenged this and asked myself, 'Why do I want to die rich?' Why do I want to work so hard, make and save so much money, only to die rich? It does not make sense.

After making a few values assessment, it finally became clear to me that *rich* was not the word I was looking for. All my life, I thought this was what I was searching for. I tried to define *rich*, and it did not sit well with me or who I am.

I found that people who are seen as rich are those who have high income, lavish lifestyles, careless spending and luxurious possessions. They have expensive taste in all things that can be seen and judged by the outside world, including massive mansions, high-end luxury vehicles, signature clothing, premium quality watches, branded bags, expensive shoes, shining jewellery and accessories that showcase status and shout 'I am rich'.

They possess items defining what the rich are all about, and they carry these as statements of personal style and achievement. It is both an entitlement and a reward that rich people give themselves to define and be distinguished from those who are not like them in their exclusive environments.

I observed what rich was like within my own circle of family – obsessed, insensitive, narcissistic, full of ego, try-hard, attention seeking, always engaging in wealthy competition with the Joneses. High income, massive mortgage, buried in debt, lots of depreciating assets and very low net worth may be some secrets that they keep.

We are not in the category of the rich. We didn't have high income, and our spending was and continues to be carefully planned, often frugal and strategic. Our possessions are minimal, mostly inexpensive and do not define us or our self-worth.

What we own are appreciating assets. We focus on a debt-free life. Our goal is a peaceful, healthy, sustainable lifestyle based on financial independence, freedom and choice. What I was searching for was a growing net worth that allows us to live stress-free, be healthy, spend quality time with loved ones, build solid relationships, engage in meaningful and leisurely activities (like travel, hobbies, music and sports), contribute, add value and leave a legacy.

That is when I changed my mindset to say: **I want to live wealthy**!

I no longer care if I die poor. If I'm dead, what would I want this wealth for? I have defined what wealth is all about – make use of my wealth and live a fulfilled, happy life.

Retirement is at any age. The FIRE (Financial Independence, Retire Early) movement has seen men and women in their 30s and 40s

(20s even) leave the workforce and retire. That is the time in their lives when they do something they love or are passionate about. In my 60s, I am too late for FIRE. This is not early. But FI is still very important.

Net worth

Let's face it. Money is important. It touches every aspect of human life. When talking about wealth, the first thing that comes to mind is financial freedom – freedom to buy what we need and what we want without restrictions within our comfortable capacity. I'm not talking about a Learjet or a luxury yacht; I'm talking about having adequate provisions and a long-term, sustainable financial foundation.

Wealth automatically makes people think of money. So, what is money? Is that wealth? Money is a part of wealth. Net worth is the total summary of all our assets (money in the bank, liquid and digital investments, properties, vehicles, jewellery, valuable collectibles, personal belongings) less all our debts, loans, payables and financial commitments. Living wealthy is having a healthy net worth, consistently growing in value, that will support your lifestyle of choice.

Money is important, most especially in retirement when we are no longer actively working for money. We aim to passively create value, meaning that even when we are sleeping or doing nothing, our money is working to make more money for us.

At retirement, our spending budget shifts from basic food, utilities, clothing and shelter to medical expenses, insurance, replacement costs, and bucket list items that include passions and hobbies.

By this time, hopefully, retirees would have paid off their home mortgage and would no longer be spending a big chunk of their income on accommodation. This is the biggest part of the budget that people, retirees or not, deal with.

The biggest advice all financial planners give is to pay off the mortgage first. This is our ticket to financial freedom. Not only will we reduce our biggest expense, it will also help us increase the value of our net worth.

During retirement, I found that there are so many maintenance and replacement costs. If you own a home, house repairs and maintenance are never-ending – roof repairs, painting, plumbing, garden, electricals and general cleaning. Home appliances break down every few years. Living wealthy means having the provisions to replace your refrigerator, washing machine, dryer, heaters or air conditioners and other small appliances without financial hardship.

If you are renting, hopefully you have saved and invested enough money from not having a mortgage, which should now be earning passive income for you.

Electronic devices are essentials and indispensable these days. Ensure you are updated with technology without the stress of having to find the money to pay for these.

Wealthy living means having no restrictions on some splurges (not lifestyle creep), including clothing, footwear, dining out, optional business class travel, hobbies, celebrations, personal services (such as cleaning, gardening, massage), gift-giving and, most especially, donations and family support.

In terms of medical expenses, Australia is one of the best countries in the world in providing universal health care to its citizens and permanent residents. We are so blessed that we are here in this lucky country. Australians enjoy one of the longest life expectancies in the world due to the quality of life and health care.

Regardless, I still see many clients who are affected by medical issues and rare conditions that are not covered by Medicare. Medical expenses are definitely something to prepare, plan and watch out for. Wealthy living means we must have adequate insurance or savings provisions for this.

I have heard horror stories of uninsured people paying thousands of dollars for ambulance services, medical tests, professional fees or hospital bills in other countries. I have witnessed firsthand, many times, families and friends in the Philippines fundraising for hospital bills and funeral expenses.

We all know money is important. Wealthy living is being aware of our relationship with money, and that relationship should work for us and our needs.

Limiting beliefs and a wealthy mindset

What is money? What is wealth? What is our relationship with money?

I find that some of my clients, even some of my friends and family, have a mindset of, 'I want to limit my income so I don't have to pay a lot of tax, and I want to be entitled to government pension/ welfare (Centrelink).' This is a limiting belief that can have serious consequences. This is a subconscious intention to say, 'I am not prepared to have overflowing money. I do not want abundance in my life. I limit my income within the threshold so that I can receive government pension. I am not prepared to pay taxes.'

Sometimes, limiting beliefs such as this can obstruct our ability to attract money instead of opening possibilities for abundance. We have a relationship with money that we need to be aware of.

In my financial literacy sessions, I ask my clients, 'What money mindset do you have? Are you careful with money? Are you mindful of how it should be used? Are you ready to own an abundance of money?'

Money is described by some as energy – it comes and it goes. Money is a representation of value created. We should not limit our thinking when it comes to creating more money and creating more value. The abundance mindset does not entertain and support limiting beliefs. If you subconsciously think of and focus on the lack of money or lack of sources of money or limited money, you will manifest this in your life.

You can reframe your focus and have a positive attraction to wealth and abundance thinking by saying, 'I am grateful for all the wealth that I have and is coming to me. Money flows to me from known and unknown sources because I add value and provide service to others.'

Trust that the energy you send out will be the same energy that will come back to you. My experience is that once I send out that energy of creating value, circumstances, people and opportunities magically arrive to me, as if telling me and supporting me in my quest to create more value.

Money is a consequence of value, and I sincerely believe that money flows where value goes.

For me, paying taxes is another way to give back. Do not demonise tax. When I pay more taxes, I am adding more value. It means I made more money, so there is nothing wrong with paying more taxes. Once you say, 'I don't want to pay more taxes', it is almost equivalent to saying, 'I don't want to create more value or create more money.'

The reason I am saying this is that if we plan to rely only on a government pension, on a practical level, retiring comfortably may not be achievable. Don't let government regulations control our happy retirement. Let's have a self-funded retirement plan that we have control of to live a lifestyle of our choice. Think of a government pension as a supplement rather than your primary source of income.

Never limit your mindset to what can possibly flow in your life abundantly.

Time

Time is wealth. Some people have a lot of money, but they are time-poor. They can't even enjoy the money they have because they are too busy doing many things. People can measure their net worth and know how much they have. But people don't know how much time they have left.

Being able to spend your time the way you want is one of the greatest joys of life, a true measure of living wealthy. Spending time with yourself, your family, your friends, doing things that you love or doing work that heaven has assigned for you to do is such a privilege when you have financial independence. You can do something or do nothing and still be equally happy.

Time is a God-given privilege on our spiritual journey to have as much human experience as possible. People always say, 'Live life to the fullest.' But what is the fullest when you do not have financial independence?

When properly balanced, health, time and money are a perfect trifecta that can enable living life to the fullest. In my desire to share my personal experience in winning this trifecta, I created a health-time-money diagram with hints on each intersecting section (Diagram 1). I also created my abundance triangle in achieving this trifecta (Diagram 2). We need to believe and create this perfect trifecta in our quest to live a full life. It is important to set an intention to find this sweet spot in our spiritual timeline to achieve this. Equilibrium in all things is something I learned from my mum.

'Just do everything in moderation and in good intention,' she would say. Be patient. The time will come when everything will be perfectly in place.

Lesson 10: There is a time for everything.
– Ecclesiastes 3:1-8

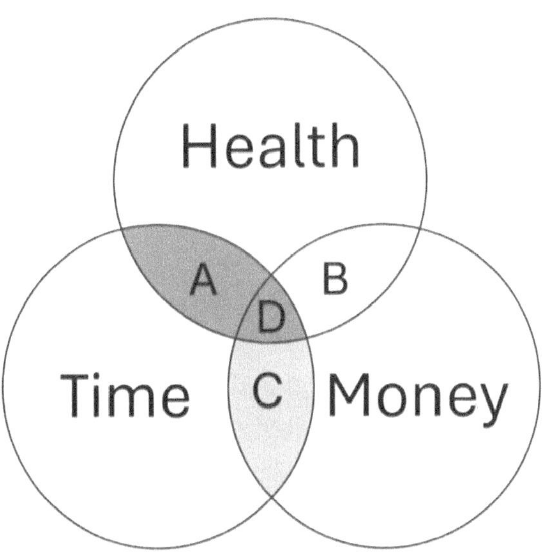

My trifecta tips on intersecting spaces:

(A) Time + Health

- Create mental wealth.
- Learn and build new skills.
- Nurture your creativity.
- Explore financial literacy.
- Start a savings plan and build an emergency fund.
- Set life goals – health, career, relationships, financial, emotional and mental wellbeing.

(B) Health + Money

- Live a healthy lifestyle with long-term health goals.
- Invest in personal growth and career progression.
- Clarify your calling and purpose.
- Build meaningful relationships.
- Master financial literacy.
- Build your net worth.

- Pay off debts.
- Maximise time factor by investing in low-cost, long-term liquid assets with little or no admin management required. Consistently top up your investment accounts and/or superannuation.

(C) Time + Money
- Prioritise physical health and wellness. Choose an appropriate exercise.
- Eat healthy food and be mindful of your diet.
- Have quality sleep. Keep moving.
- Boost mental agility.
- Spend time with loved ones.
- Stay socially engaged.
- Embrace change.

(D) Time + Health + Money
- Let gratitude be your guide.
- Celebrate life. Fulfill your dreams.
- Live your passion. Engage in new experiences.
- Travel. Explore the world. Learn more.
- Enjoy financial independence through passive income.
- Be generous. Pay forward. Contribute.
- Inspire others. Leave a legacy.

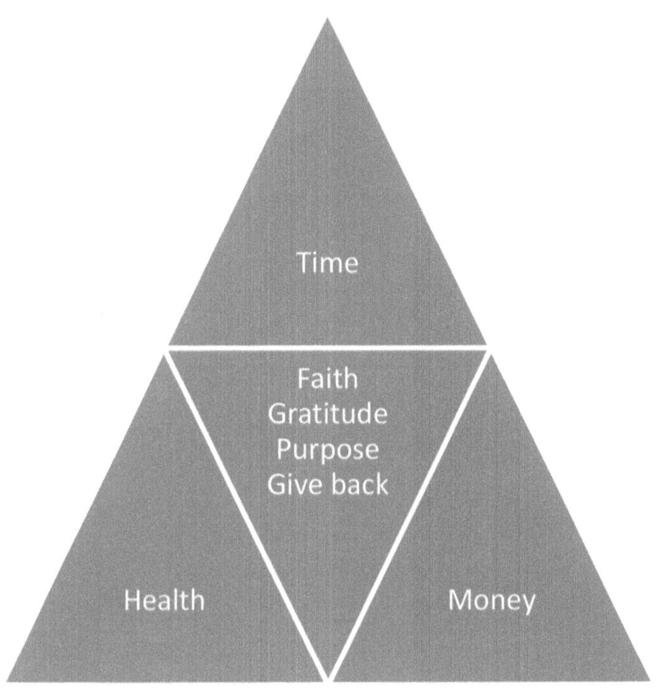

My Abundance Triangle – We achieve a sweet trifecta of balancing time, health and money when in the core of our spirituality, we accept that we are spiritual beings having a human experience. We are not human beings having a spiritual experience. Build a life on a foundation of faith, gratitude, purpose and giving back.

11

Guided by gratitude and prayer

Gratitude is the healthiest of all human emotions. The more you express gratitude for what you have, the more likely you will have even more to express gratitude for.
— Zig Ziglar

Prayer is power. We grew up in a family where our constant is prayer. Mum and Dad have raised us in prayers. Growing up, we used to pray the Holy Rosary every day as a family. In school, we started with our morning prayers, Angelus at lunchtime and prayers before going home. We went to mass every Sunday and all holidays of obligation. When we embark on new projects, whether large or small, we pray for guidance. When we're at crossroads, we pray. When we need strength to carry on, we pray. When we have answered prayers, we say prayers of gratitude.

My grandma's sister taught me how to pray. She said, 'When you pray, you **STOP. S**: Say sorry for your shortcomings and misgivings. **T**: Thank and be grateful. **O**: Offer your work, sacrifice, your life. Give. **P**: Petition. Ask for whatever is the desire of your heart, but say Thy will be done.'

I had a workmate who could not understand this. She said she grew up in this kind of environment, never knowing how to pray or what it is all about. She just does what she thinks is good and right. Oftentimes, she gets it wrong, and most times she is unlucky. She once said to me that she wished she knew the way I used prayer in my daily life because she noticed that I always get better outcomes than her.

I am not one who memorises verses from the Bible or argues with anyone to impose my own beliefs, but I have so much faith in the power of prayers. I just STOP. It's usually a quiet whisper to the divine spirits, 'Please guide me through. Without you, I am weak. Without your light, I am in darkness.'

Throughout our major crossroads, I can say that we have been guided. I always start with gratitude — the key to abundance. It is when we say thank you before we receive, that we are given more. It is when we ask to bless our path to be lit with grace so we can serve. It is when we have unwavering faith and trust that we embrace our human experiences to live a life of abundance.

God has been so gracious in guiding us. From the many earthquakes of different kinds in my life, to the car accidents that I survived or have missed, to the wars and revolutions I personally witnessed, to the fire that gutted the whole apartment complex and spared Apartment C, where we lived — I have been blessed.

To all the illnesses and medical episodes I survived, which let me intentionally create a mindset of a healthy lifestyle and conscious awareness to look after my physical body and wellbeing. To my near-drowning experience at 10 years old, which allowed me to yearn to learn how to swim and now enables me to have my most enjoyable healthy routine of swimming 1,200 metres a week.

From the difficult days at school, trying to blend in with my privileged classmates, to my childhood envy of not being able to eat caramel popcorn, get a balloon at the churchyard or have a Sunday lunch at Aristocrat restaurant have built compassion for my clients and sincerely understand what a child goes through when listening to their stories of hardship.

Everything happened in divine, perfect timing.

My first job in Rorer Philippines provided me with the platform not only to launch my career in finance but also to create a lifelong relationship with the most inspiring individuals I call My Rorer family. My first real mentor was our marketing manager. He taught us life lessons in financial literacy, always reminding us, 'Have at least six months of money buffer. In case anything happens to you, you know you can survive the next six months.' and 'Be careful with your spending. Make sure you have good investments for the future. Live a life of simplicity. Choose a good partner in life.'

That time when my miracle baby was born, we were buried in so much debt. There was much physical pain, so much stress from not knowing – that was a blessed time when God showed His grace and mercy. It was a time when we realised who our real friends were. Our friends, in the kindness of their hearts, rallied behind us, fundraising to get us through the hardship. It made a stressful life a lot easier, knowing that there was so much support and love regardless of the amount of money raised.

It was also a miraculous time. There was so much business coming in. Our little software business experienced that big boom; we had to employ a few more programmers, and we were able to pay for the hospital bills.

That was living proof for me that when God gives you challenges to complete your puzzle, He also sends the right people to show up. Amidst the chaos, He gives you the right circumstances to put your puzzle pieces together in some orderly fashion.

The time when I was made redundant from work left me anxious about my next steps towards life. What was I going to do from here? How do I proceed? It allowed my family to have time to close our business, allowed me to go on holiday to spend time with my family in California and allowed us to have money to start our migration to Australia.

Timing was perfect.

Oh, I forgot to mention an unbelievable bonus when I took my little niece to the US. The flight was fully booked, and we were going to be bumped off. Instead, the airline upgraded us to business class going to LA! It was my first business class experience, as if heaven said, 'This is it. Relax. No need for anxiety. Prepare to live wealthy!'

My wonderful aunt and uncle, who invited, sponsored and welcomed us in Australia, served as our guide, our mentors, our inspiration. My aunt is a living saint, and I always wish I could even be half the person that she is, knowing that I will never even be that close.

She's the aunt that everyone looks up to in our family. She's the sister my dad (and everyone else – siblings, nephews, nieces, in-laws) always went to for support when in trouble. I knew she secretly provided financial assistance to our family when we were growing up. She looks after her neighbour, delivering hot food or caring for them when they're unwell. She always has time for everyone – her friends, her colleagues at church and just about anyone who needs her help – despite her busy schedule with the demands of a fulltime nurse and a mother of five.

She's the church lady who quietly volunteers for everything and anything to help run the parish. She helped put up a shrine of San Lorenzo Ruiz, the first Filipino saint, in the sacred grounds of Penrose Park, Berrima, 150 kilometres from Sydney. She has so much dedication and commitment to keep and religiously maintain the shrine despite her old age.

She is not only my aunt but a sacred soul and angel on earth that God gave me.

I realised later on that I was subconsciously following my aunt's path. I found out that we went to the same university. When looking at her wedding photos, where I was her flower girl, I discovered that we got married in the same church, even though we lived nowhere near that parish. Unbelievable as it is, we were also blessed by the same priest at our wedding, 19 years apart. She married an engineer, and so did I. I followed her to Australia.

It is with God's divine guidance and grace that I am given the right people to follow and be inspired by.

That tiny voice of prayer of my miracle baby, saying, 'God, please help my dad find work,' and Eric humbly asking for guidance, 'Lord, please help me find what is mine,' eventually landing him a job at Microsoft and being our first step in building Eric's career and life as new migrants in Australia.

The bank's letter telling us that we cannot pay off our loan early, then we had to be creative in what to do to avoid huge penalty fees forced us to research and gave us the idea of starting our first investment in index funds and ETFs.

The year 2008 provided miracles, healing, forgiveness and peace, my mum's 75th birthday, our pilgrimage to Lourdes, my second redundancy, finding my new career in counselling – everything was in perfect divine order.

The second redundancy on 08/08/2008, a date of significance in Asian numerology – the number 8 signifying balance, abundance, cosmic order, and good fortune – was our investment boost during the worst slump since the Great Depression. We invested at a perfectly low point in the share market during the global financial crisis. On this day, how was it possible that I found financial counselling as if it was dropped in front of me to have the work that heaven assigned for me?

I was given access to a free, fully funded course, with transport and food allowance to study financial counselling. It opened doors for me to restart a new career to fulfill my intention to serve and add value, combining finance, human behaviour, community work and some paralegal aspects.

At my dad's dying bedside, I whispered in his ear, 'Dad, I am no longer working as a CPA. I now work to serve the community, and there are some paralegal aspects to my job.'

He smiled in his state of almost comatose. I knew he was happy. I was no longer bean-counting. It was important to him that we do community service as part of our lives. God's time was on point once again.

My mum's teachings on praying 'Lord, thy will be done' when she apologised for kneel-walking to request a baby boy – this has been our faithful prayer, trusting that He has plans we may not see or cannot understand yet but is a part of our life puzzle to complete.

All my insecurities about being born poor are now my greatest motivation and human experience to move forward, get people inspired, live a wealthy life and dream about less poverty in the world.

All the hurt and rage I felt over my dad's indiscretion to my mum and all the vengeful thinking replaced by forgiveness, peace and gratitude at the baths in Lourdes is now the greatest blessing. Meeting my sister Liz is one of the most amazing graces that God has showered me. Almost always, there is a rainbow that shows up to remind me of this.

My great frustration of not being able to study in my dream university, the University of the Philippines (UP), for the only reason that we could not afford daily public transport to that university, and eventually obtaining a scholarship at the Philippine Women's University (PWU), my mum's preferred university, because it was so much closer to home and because PWU is her alma mater. This is the institution that allowed me to meet my true best friends and Eric. I found out later that he was going to enrol in UP but decided to go to a specialised engineering university.

God's divine plan was for us to meet in a student leadership camp. I always think that having my wonderful husband is my greatest wealth and happiness. What if I went to UP? Would our paths have crossed? Would my life have been different?

My pieces to my puzzle are slowly being put together. As if an invisible force has always been there for me, I have been guided.

For all these, I am so grateful. Gratitude is the key that unlocks abundance.

Sayang

Sayang is a Filipino word that has no exact English equivalent. Filipinos use it in so many different ways and circumstances. It can be defined as:

- an expression of regret for a missed opportunity. For instance, when someone is in the finals for a competition but someone else won, we say, '*Sayang*, you didn't win the competition.'
- a declaration of a wasteful behaviour.
    - For people throwing out good food, we say, '*Sayang*. Don't throw away good food.
    - When a person is not mindful of limited resources (keeping the tap on while brushing their teeth), we say, '*Sayang* ang tubig.' ('Don't waste water.')
- a verbalisation of emotional support. For instance, when a long-term relationship ends in bitter divorce, we say, '*Sayang*, they had many good years together.'
- a voice of hope and encouragement. For instance, when a person is almost giving up on a project or passion when it seems to be too difficult or unsustainable, a supportive person would say, 'Come on, keep going. *Sayang*, you've done so much. Not long to go and you'll be there.'
- a value of preservation or sentimental value. When one wants to keep things (whether big, small, valuable or

otherwise) and finds it hard to let go for whatever reason, that person would say, '*Sayang*, this has been an important part of me, I can't let it go. I'll keep it.'

- to vent out regret for non-action. When a person did not pursue his passion and in old age, regrets what could have, would have, should have, we say, '*Sayang*. If only I pursued my career in music, I would have been a successful artist by now.'

- a sigh of disappointment. For instance, when a person is careless and caused an unwanted outcome, we say, 'Sayang, we could have prevented that accident from happening if we were more mindful.'

Every day, millions of Filipinos say *sayang*. The closest English group of words that could be used for *sayang* is 'What a shame' or 'What a waste'.

My late father-in-law would regularly express his regret in life, always saying *sayang*. '*Sayang*, I didn't immigrate to the USA when I had the opportunity in the 1960s.'

'*Sayang*, I wish I pursued my dream to be a pilot.'

'*Sayang*, I wish I didn't have to close down my tailoring business.'

My friend expressed regret when she found out the unit price of the ETF I recommended had grown from $200 to $450 over five years, when I encouraged her to buy some shares. '*Sayang,* I should have followed your lead. If I bought 100 shares then, I would have more than doubled my portfolio of at least $45,000 now.'

In 2019, we spent time with Eric's cousin and his wife in their annual Holy Thursday procession of saints. They had been so busy with their many businesses and were still thinking of venturing into more diverse businesses. They have a beautiful, big house in one of the exclusive villages in Manila, a good net worth and a continuing income stream.

His wife told me she dreams of travelling to Lourdes, France, but they are too busy managing their business. I told her that they should make time, if that is important to her. 'We are in our retirement age, and this is the time to slowly turn our dreams into reality.'

Soon, they were planning to travel in a few years. The next year, in 2020, we got the shocking news that her husband was one of the early casualties of COVID and died alone in the isolation room. He was returned to them in an urn. Unfortunately, her dream of travelling to France with her beloved husband never materialised. *Sayang.* They missed the trifecta of health-time-money balance to enjoy the fruits of their labour.

During our annual Easter week celebration, my cousin's husband, with four young children under 8 years old, suddenly had a stroke and dropped dead in front of everyone. He didn't know he had a medical condition because he wasn't having regular medical check-ups. *Sayang,* only if he had known his medical condition, early intervention could have been done.

My client was happily married for 30 years but suddenly told me that they are getting a divorce. She said, '*Sayang,* life is too short to pretend that I am happily married. I need to move on to heal and enjoy the remaining years of my life.'

I lost my dear friend of 34 years while I was writing this memoir, when she lost her battle with cancer. Her only sibling, whom she longed to spend time with for many years, lives in LA. The first and only time her brother came to visit her in Sydney was when their mother died in 2007. She told her brother then, 'Why did you come to visit only now? How many times did Mum ask you to come over here so we can bond as a family?'

Her brother regretted that he was here for their mother's funeral instead of spending happy times together while she was still alive.

In the hospital where my friend was in palliative care, lying almost lifeless, her brother once again turned up, just arrived from LA. I told him, 'You did this when your mum passed away 18 years ago. Here we are again.'

We never learn our lesson.

He whispered in her ear, 'Sister, I am so sorry,' quietly hoping that she heard him.

Family, friends and clients alike say this word – *sayang*.

Sayang, I should have finished my college education or trade qualification and could have had more chances of success in life, if only I had listened to my parents and heeded their advice.

Sayang, we could have saved enough money if my partner and I hadn't spent it on gambling.

Sayang, I didn't build my superannuation and retirement fund.

Sayang, I wish I had spent more time with my friend or my sister if I had known she had a terminal illness.

In my research, I found out that *sayang* is also a word used in Malaysia, Singapore and Indonesia. It is a verb that means 'to love'. It is also a noun – a term of endearment for someone loved so dearly. At the other end of the continuum, it also means pity and waste.

'One day, any day, last day' has been my recent mantra in living my daily life. Today could be that one day, any day, last day. I live not in fear but in the awareness of my unknown one day, any day, last day. It makes me think of what is really important in life and focus on it. Is it money? Is it passion and purpose? Is it health? Is it great relationships?

Retirement is that special time to reflect. It is an opportunity to reassess. It is the last homecoming stretch to the finish line. It is time to do all that I wished I had done before. Live life without any regrets and don't say any more *sayang*.

I ask myself if I have managed all the *sayangs* in my life at this stage in the context of regret, waste, meaning and purpose.

Declutter and detach

Towards the end of my writing, I think to myself if I have leftover *sayangs*, if there's anything unresolved within my heart, if I have truly lived a wealthy life, if I have done everything in my power and control to find those extra missing pieces of my puzzle. As always, I pray for guidance.

Yes, I have leftover *sayangs*. Now is my time to tick off my bucket list. It is also my time to declutter and free myself from all that no longer serve me. Time to let go of stuff lying around the house. Time to let go of investments that are not doing well. Time to let go of toxic relationships that are not bearing fruit. Time to let go of the past that has contributed to my life puzzle but is no longer relevant to my inner peace.

I am writing this book because I don't want to say in my old age one day, '*Sayang*, I wish I had written a book to share my story. Who knows if it may serve as a flicker of hope and light to someone who might find their story in mine, or someone who may learn something from my own life lessons?'

Retirement is that special time to detach from who we think we are and remember that we are not human havings and human doings; we are human beings. If, in retirement, you still identify yourself with what you have (I have a massive mansion; I have a luxury car; I have all these signature clothing, branded shoes, bags and jewelleries; I have millions of dollars; I have nothing) or find your self-worth in what you do or how you are valued by society (I am a doctor. I am a judge. I am a CEO. I am a General. I am a president. I am a school principal. I am a rockstar. I am an accomplished athlete. I am a famous celebrity. I am a homeless destitute.), you may find yourself lost. This is the best time to tune in to your values, beliefs and perspective.

Be. Just be.

Life is too short to say *sayang*. Live wealthy. Retire happy.

Lesson 11: A musician must make music. An artist must paint. A poet must write, if he is to be ultimately at peace with himself. – Abraham Maslow

---

12

Amazing moments
of grace

In the end, it's not the years in your life
that count. It's the life in your years.
– Abraham Lincoln

Most year-ends, I write a short journal of the year that has been.
It is a reminder of my wealthy living. I will share some journals at
the end of the chapters of my wealthy living, having wonderful
relationships, a healthy lifestyle and financial independence.

In this final chapter, I will invite you to attend my pretend 100th
birthday. As in life, death is also something we plan for. 'Do not be
a burden,' says my mum.

Client case:
Male, 78 years old, single, living alone, works part-time as an
Uber driver, receives Centrelink pension, has no significant assets.
Wants to see me for concerns about his funeral insurance that he
has been paying for over 15 years. He estimates that he has now
paid close to $10,000 over this period.

He asked the insurance company if he had any benefits at this time, only to find out that the insurance he signed up for is for his beneficiary when he dies. As he is alone in his life, he has no family or beneficiary and was shocked to find out that it was not the funeral insurance he wanted. He did not understand what he signed up for and is now confused as to what to do. He wants to make sure he will be taken care of when he dies and not be a burden.

I explained to my client that there is a difference between funeral insurance and funeral bonds. Funeral insurance provides a lump sum payout for beneficiaries upon death. Funeral bonds are investment products to help save up for funeral expenses.

Retirement years can be daunting when we are running out of time, running out of physical strength/energy and running out of money – maybe even running out of friends, family and social connections. If you are retiring after 60, like me, it can also be your time of reflection, thinking of the years behind you. Did I live a full life of meaning and purpose? What great relationships did I invest in, build and cherish the most? Do I have any regrets? How will I be remembered? Did I make the world more beautiful and good?

If you are retiring early, like FIRE, it can be the time to look forward to asking yourself, 'What full life am I ready to live? What great relationships should I build and invest in? What new activities excite, motivate and fill my life with joy that I need to pursue and spend my time, energy and resources with? What gives me the most satisfaction and fulfillment?'

As in life, planning is imperative in death. My children have once joked, 'Mum, since you already planned for your end of life, maybe you can also plan to write your own eulogy.'

I thought it was funny, and we all laughed. But later, I realised that there is value in this. Writing your own eulogy gives you an ultimate goal to ask yourself the question: What will be the narrative at the end of my life? Did I live my life the way I wanted to? How many of my dreams did I fulfill? What stopped me from fulfilling all of my dreams? What wonderful human experience was I blessed with? What am I grateful for?

Writing your own eulogy makes you think of how you want to share your life puzzle pieces to those you love.

It freaked me out. The thing with eulogies is that we speak about someone who cannot hear the good things we say about them. When I attend funerals and eulogies, I say to myself, 'If only the dead can hear. Why only now? I wish they had said those wonderful tributes when he was alive. It would be heartwarming to hear those lovely words.'

What is the point? Eulogies are for the living and not for the dead.

I remember in 2022, immediately after the COVID lockdown, we travelled to San Francisco to visit my mum, who was seriously ill from the effects of COVID. In great fear that we were going to lose Mum very soon, we organised a family event to celebrate her life. Everyone had to do a speech about my mum – like a eulogy, but to the living.

We said all the good memories we shared with her. Some stories were funny inside jokes, some were about her teachings and how they impacted our lives and some were trivia Q&As. It was a great gathering of family with so much love and laughter. Even with dementia, Mum loved every part of it. We all loved it.

So, instead of a eulogy, let me invite you to my pretend 100th birthday in 2062. I may have some form of physical incapacity by then, perhaps dementia. My best friend or my aged care service provider will be delivering this speech.

100th birthday speech

We are gathered here today to celebrate 100 years of the life of Maria Corazon Uranza Zamora Cardenas. Her name recognises her mother, her father and her husband – the three people who are most dear to her heart. Her recognition of those who have made a significant impact on her life is typical of her.

She is fondly called Cora by those close to her, and Ate Tatts, Aunty Tatts or Tatta by those closest to her. At 100, we can say that she has lived a full life.

Today, she is with her dear husband, Eric, and two wonderful sons, Craig and Egon and their families. She dedicated her life to her family. Everything she did was for the love of her family so they could be proud of her and the work she did. Her mission statement is to live a life that her parents would be proud of and her children and grandchildren would be inspired by.

Although Cora was educated in an exclusive private girls' school and university, she had humble beginnings with working-class parents. She earned her university degree in business administration through a college scholarship at the Philippine Women's University and graduated with distinction. She earned her master's degree in business management at the Macquarie Graduate School of Management in Sydney, sponsored by Pfizer while working there.

Cora had a successful corporate finance career for 25 years as a CPA. She is a highly regarded counsellor and a published author. Her last remaining years before full retirement were dedicated to serving the community in her capacity as an advocate, financial counsellor and financial literacy educator.

She is known to have a passion for helping people and making a difference in their lives. Cora is a modest, simple, average, ordinary human being who achieved extraordinary outcomes. There are countless family, friends and clients whom she supported to ease their financial burden as well as contributed immensely towards their health and wellbeing. She provided life-changing experiences to many through her advocacy, dedication and research.

She believes in spirituality and in things that are not of this world. She is very grateful for the human experiences she embraced, as they provided her with the platform and literary material she needed to publish her successful manuscripts.

She lives a simple, humble life. Her possessions are few, not valuable, but priceless. When once asked, 'What do you collect?', her response was, 'Thank you notes, thank you emails, thank you drawings from little children, and thank you hugs.'

She never forgot her humble beginnings as the daughter of a poor farmer's son. At 100, she is continuing to support and help those who need her assistance.

Cora never bought expensive things for herself. Instead, she gave away her wealth to help those less fortunate than her.

In her younger years, she enjoyed a healthy lifestyle and built amazing relationships. You are all here today because you are part of her network of true friends, whose lives she has touched, who stood by her side, who have been inspired by her and who shared her joy in celebrating her wins.

Her relationship with Eric continues to be an envy to all. They recently celebrated their wedding anniversary – 77 wonderful years of love, life and learning. Together, they continue to share a full and joyful life. They fill their days with simple and healthy activities like walking, swimming, music and fun day outs with many of you here today.

Until their mid- to late 80s, they travelled at least once a year to see and enjoy the rest of the world. She kept physically healthy to enjoy her travels with Eric and with her closest friends. They have travelled to over 100 countries across all continents throughout Asia, North America, Europe, South America, Africa, Antarctica and across the Pacific Islands, including Australia and New Zealand. She spoke a few languages, enjoyed learning about different cultures, history, geography, food, music and human behaviour.

Eric and Cora raised two wonderful sons, Craig and Egon. Both of them have obtained university degrees and are recognised for their significant contributions in the fields of creative writing and finance, respectively.

Cora is a woman of grace, compassion, integrity, honour, kindness, humility and strength. She serves as a role model and as an inspiration to those whose lives she touched, beginning from the impoverished city of Manila to the wealthy leafy suburb of Dural in northwestern Sydney. Cora is highly respected and well loved by her siblings, cousins, nephews, nieces, friends, clients, colleagues and business partners. Eric, her sons and their families congratulate her today on this special milestone not everyone is privileged to have.

Thank you very much to all of you for sharing this momentous day.

Truth or consequence

Is this true? Is this what my best friend will say about me? Will I even get to 100 or travel to 100 countries or celebrate our 77th wedding anniversary or speak a few languages? Not yet. Or maybe not at all.

But why focus on what might not happen? I remembered my mentor when I was reviewing for my CPA board exams. He always said, 'Focus on being number one. Aim for the top spot. Imagine when the results of the CPA board exams are released, your name is in the number one position.'

All of us in our review class, thousands of us, aimed for the top spot. Why? Our mentor made it clear. 'If you do not get the top spot, maybe you will be number two or maybe in the top 10 or top 100 or top 1,000. If you do not get in any of these spots, maybe you would at least pass the CPA. Pass is good. If you aim only for *Pass* and you do not achieve this, it means you will fail. Always aim for a top spot, and you will work towards a good outcome.'

There is some truth to some of the narratives in my 100th birthday speech. I will keep building on that. This is the ultimate goal – believing that this is my top spot I wish to become. If I ever get to 100 years of age, this is what I wish to hear – that I have done and who I became. This is what I wish to share to those with me in the room. People always ask 100-year-olds during their birthday, 'What's your secret?'

My sister, Aldrina always reminds me of The 7 Habits of Highly Effective People by Stephen R. Covey. Habit number two: Begin with the end in mind. That's the secret.

Begin to write about your 100th birthday celebration **now** as you read my book. Imagine all your friends and family in a wonderful venue. Imagine all the wonderful things you have achieved over your lifetime. Imagine how, through your hard work, you have touched people's lives and inspired all these people in the room. Imagine that you have been living the life of your dreams.

This is your chance to visualise and create that end in mind. Define what wealth of experience you would be sharing to all. Identify what is really important to you. Focus on what sparks joy and what truly makes you happy. Begin today.

Live wealthy. Retire Happy!

Lesson 12: Begin with gratitude. Allow abundance to flow. Create a fulfilling life of meaning and purpose by visualising and focusing on your ultimate goal.

Journals

December 2008

Mum's 75th birthday

I come from a poor background. As I was growing up I saw how much mum sacrificed herself and her life for our whole family. Mum was a school teacher but ended up being a stay-at-home mum to look after her six children. Everyday, my mum would wash our clothes with her bare hands. I saw how her hands would oftentimes be infected, bleed, crack and separate from the nail bed from the constant exposure to laundry detergent. At one point, I saw her fingernails all gone. They have all been eaten up with infection. Even with this condition, she continued washing clothes day in and day out without fail. But she never complained about it.

I saw all her hardships – financial hardships, physical hardships, psychological hardships, emotional hardships, spiritual hardships. All through my life, I swear, I would do everything I can to make mum happy. I wanted to improve the quality of her life.

I was just an average kid so I had average outcomes in life. I studied, finished my degree, found a job, I got married and started my own family. I got busy with my own family. I had my own challenges to face. My mum and I got separated when she migrated to USA to join my sister and I migrated to Australia. I never got the chance to show my love for my mum in the way I wanted to show her. It was constantly on my mind to do something for my mum to show my love for her.

After 25 years of working full time, my job was made redundant on 08/08/08. At first, I was overly anxious of this unfortunate event. But as the spiritual person that I am, I took it as a blessing. I took this opportunity to spend time with my mum and just be with her. I learned that she wanted to go on a religious pilgrimage to Europe. With the time off and redundancy money I got, I quickly organised a trip to France and Italy with my mum and sister.

The timing was so perfect. It was the 150th anniversary of the apparition of the Lady of Lourdes. There was a big celebration happening in Lourdes, France. I didn't realise that this was mum's life long dream – to join this pilgrimage. There must be a guiding spirit that's leading me.

When we got to Lourdes, France the celebration date was 13th of September to 8th of December. That was the fi rst sign of our amazing synchronicity! 13th of September was mum and dad's wedding anniversary and 8th of December is mum's birthday! Coincidence?

We travelled to France and Italy. We had the most fantastic experience and we enjoyed every single bit of our travel. A special mention of our sacred and phenomenal time at the Baths of Lourdes where mum, sis and myself immersed in the holy baths and came out dry. At the end of the pilgrimage, we visited my auntie who is a nun in Rome. We didn't know it was my auntie's 65th birthday! It was another perfect timing! My auntie was so happy we celebrated her birthday milestone with her. And my mum was so happy to be with my auntie who she hasn't seen for a very long time. It was a great trip. We had a great time.

We returned to San Francisco in late November. This was the year when my mum was turning 75 years old. In December, we organised a big 75th birthday party for mum with all her friends. But 8th of

December was on a Monday, so we held the big party on the 6th of December, Saturday. My mum's speech on her birthday was one with overwhelming happiness. I remember her saying about her sacrifices, her rotten fingernails, her hardships, struggles and success. But all these will come to an end, she said. She couldn't believe all the blessings she has been given – 75 wonderful years of love from family and friends. She says: What a way to celebrate a 75th birthday: to finally realise a dream trip of a lifetime and end with a big party with family and friends. She didn't know there was more to come.

On Monday, the 8th of December, we were planning to attend mass at the local parish to simply celebrate mum's birthday. Suddenly, Fr. August Villote, our close friend/ mum's pseudo son, parish priest from San Francisco calls us to let us know that a healing priest, Fr. Fernando Suarez, is visiting from the Philippines. He is so well known, people camp out 2-3 days before the event so that they can see get a secured spot to see this healing priest. Because he is so popular, it is very difficult to get to see him. People are content just to hear his voice from afar. He is known to heal cancer patients, blind people, leukemia patients, impossible and almost hopeless cases, weak people on wheel chairs would stand up, etc.

We rushed to the church and the place was fully packed. We couldn't get in. For some reason, we were led by someone to get inside the church. The only spot remaining was right in front of the altar and that was where we got to be seated. It was an amazing experience for us because people couldn't even get in and we got to sit in front. How is it possible? As Fr. Fernando comes out, we were the first family to be called. What a perfect 75th birthday present for mum!! It was an incredible spiritual experience. My dad, my sister, my mum, my husband, our children - we were healed as a family. Our physical pains were wiped out. We couldn't believe what happened. It was as if there was angel that has taken all our burden away and replaced it with a spiritual energy of love, peace and happiness.

I call it an amazing moment of grace. All these magical synchronicities – where did it come from? My redundancy money, my time off, our trip to Europe, our profound moment of peace at the baths of Lourdes, the significant dates, my auntie's birthday, my mum's birthday healing mass. Because I held in my heart my love for my mum; because of my constant thought, focus and intention to do something in return for all her sacrifices, by God's grace we were guided to help us create a beautiful human experience.

16 May 2014

My interesting day

I had my day all mapped out – go for my usual Friday swim, do my laundry, surprise my best friend, Pinky, with a quick lunch, go shopping, go for a quick bike ride with my darling hubby. After my swim, I got a text message from Pinky asking me if I wanted to have lunch with her and Ate Nida. I quickly obliged thinking that I was planning to surprise her anyway. She said they were going to church at 12 noon. We can meet at church and decide where to have lunch when we're all together.

I quickly washed up my chlorine-soaked hair and skin, packed my swimming costume, drove back home, put my first load up on the line, completed my second load and ran upstairs to quickly change for my lunch date. I headed straight to the garage to my parked car and barely said goodbye to my dear Eric. It was 11.45 am.

My car was third in line at the intersection ready to turn right with two little cars in front of me. The lights turned green and we each begin to head off. All cars in front are in full stop. To my left, all cars are also in full stop position. To my right, there were 3 lanes - There was a car waiting to turn right , The middle lane was open and the car on the further left lane was also waiting. Both the cars at the further right and further left were in full stop position. Full stop of course, their set of lights is on RED.

As I was turning, a 4-wheel drive Nissan X-Trail in the middle lane of the right side (which was originally empty) coming from the top of the hill was accelerating towards me. It was speeding as if it was coming to get me. It was an "Oh, sh*t - What the hell is the driver thinking?" moment. Your lights are RED!! STOP you idiot! Everyone's in stop position!! Just STOP!! Do you understand what RED means? It means STOP.

The two little cars in front of me got out of the way. I tried to speed up and accelerate to avoid a collision. But just enough that I don't hit the little car in front of me. The driver coming from the right side was still totally clueless on what was happening as if everything was fine. She continued to speed and accelerate.

Not a brake. Not a swerve to the left to avoid a collision. Not a single beep. Just speed, speed, speed and more speed straight towards me. JUST STOP!! Please stop!! Just step on your brakes!! What the hell are you thinking?

Everyone was watching in shock and in horror. Someone will get hurt!!! Someone will get hurt!! Someone could die. I stepped on the accelerator as hard as I can. I tried to move towards an angle not directly at the T-section where I can almost see myself smashed and crumpled. But I couldn't accelerate enough nor could I position myself enough to avoid it.

Then finally, the inevitable happens. BAM! Like a massive ton of metal, it finally drops and hits me hard, BAMM. Her 4-wheel drive crashes onto my side. The lady is still clueless. Uhm... Did I cause an accident?

My airbags deploy. Glass shattered everywhere. There were people coming to rescue me. My car, actually my dear husband's car, turns 180 degrees. I get disorientated. I am in shock. Am I still alive?

Everything was still slowly playing out frame by frame in my mind. I was thinking of how else could I have avoided it? Am I still alive? Oh, I forgot I already asked that question. But am I? I reach for my phone and pressed my dear husband's number. I cried , "I'm in a bad accident. Please come and help me." It felt like eternity waiting for him. Then, there were so many people trying to help me. I'm Peter. I'm Howard. I'm Sam. Everyone trying to get me out. Someone was knocking at my door asking : "Are you hurt? Are you ok?" Someone was yelling, "Get the ambulance. Call the police." I can see litter everywhere. I'm thinking: Am I hurt? How badly hurt?

No, I can't get hurt. I'm on my way to meet my friend. We're having lunch. It's her birthday. Then, I realize I'm still sitting inside and people are still knocking asking if there are people hurt inside the car. I start shaking and shivering and crying.

A nurse approaches me and says, "I'm Natalie. I'm a nurse. I want to help you." Another person, Kel, calls from the outside: " I saw everything how it's happened. You were on the right. The other car tried to beat a red light." I thought for awhile: "No, she didn't beat a red light. SHE FAILED TO STOP ON A CLEARLY RED LIGHT." Kel wanted to make sure I was ok. I was still inside the car. I didn't know what to do. I just sat inside praying that everything would be fine.

No, this is not how I mapped my Friday – not inside a smashed car, not in an ambulance, not in the emergency room of Hornsby Hospital, not in a hospital gown eating hospital food.

Yet, I feel lucky. Not my time yet. Tonight I gave my family a big hug and I said I love you to each of them. Circumstances could have been different. What if I never got the chance to say it today?

31 December 2014

Reflections on our 30th wedding anniversary

There, my darling husband has spilled all the beans and opened our humble wedding album for all to see on our Facebook walls. Shame, shame, shame, I say to myself. I have kept all these pictures in the vault for so many years so no one else will see except us. This is just for Eric and me to remind us of our humble beginnings. And yet, there it is today... on social media. I feel exposed.

We were too poor then. Very poor. We couldn't afford a big wedding. My mum and dad wanted to borrow money to give us a big wedding, and they could invite all their friends and all our countless number of relatives. But no. We said no. No big wedding. No loans. No burden on our parents. No pretenses. This is who we are. This is what we can afford. And this is where we will begin our journey.

We had no wedding invites. No wedding theme. No long wedding gown for me. No wedding entourage in special clothing. No bridal shower. No hair or make-up artists. No fresh flowers. No expensive jewelries. No photography or video coverage in Betamax. No souvenirs. None of these.

Eric once told me of his own version of Albert Einstein's theory of relativity $E=MC^2$ regarding energy, mass and light. He is a true engineer. I believed him. I didn't understand what it meant but he said E is for Eric. MC is for Maria Corazon. However, MC loves E, E will not only double it but will always raise it to the 2nd power. This is as romantic as my engineer could be – sounded really good and pretty exciting. So, we secretly went by our code $E=MC^2$.

But there was something more. He created another theory of relativity and applied it on our wedding day. He said: 'The amount of money you spend on your wedding is inversely proportional to the length of time the relationship will last. The quality of your wedding is not directly related to the quality of your married life.' My darling engineer even had empirical data to support his theory. Nevertheless, our relationship was never going to be about money.

My wedding dress was made by my wonderful mother-in-law. The engagement ring and the wedding bands were heirlooms given by Lola Paz. My dad's friend, Oben Co, offered his Mercedes-Benz to be our wedding car. The bouquet of orchids was from Auntie Maring's garden. My something old, something blue and something borrowed was my mum's set of blue pearl necklace. Photography was done by my cousin Roger Angara from Sydney. The most expensive item was probably my pair of shoes (also my something new) which I bought for 120 pesos at Via Venetto, quite a price tag from an upmarket shoe boutique.

Our simple wedding had all the elements of a celebration – a blessing from Father Reyes, an exchange of vows and rings, lighting of candles, covering of wedding veil, tying of the cord, presentation of wedding coins, a gathering of family and friends.

My mum wasn't totally impressed. She felt that I deserved more than this. She wanted this day to be **her proud moment.** A moment to tell her family and friends – 'Here, see my daughter. She will begin her new life today. Be impressed.'

It wasn't as she would have wanted it. Throughout the wedding there was barely a smile on her face. Very disappointed. But she didn't know $E=MC^2$.

It bothered me that my mum wasn't happy. I knew she was happy for me because I found the love of my life, my handsome prince, my engineer. But she wasn't happy that they weren't able to share this occasion with those that matter to her and dad.

Even if I stood my ground to say, *"Today is not about her. It's about me,"* for many years I struggled to get rid of this toxic thinking and my mums' unintentional emotional manipulation. And I swore to myself, *"One day I'll make mum happy."*

We had our simple lunch reception at Aberdeen Court, a popular wedding venue less than 5kms from the church. We had around 100 guests mainly close family. My friends from PWU were not really invited but they made sure they were part of our day, so they quietly snuck in (which I thoroughly enjoyed and was truly delighted). I was honestly too embarrassed to invite my friends and workmates as it was too simple. I was so anxious of being judged. This is what poverty does to people.

During the reception, we had Chinese lauriat, the wedding cake, the wedding toast and the release of the love birds as part of the celebration. No speeches of thanks, credits and acknowledgments. It wasn't the order of those days. No music. No wedding band. No bride and groom dance. No frills.

After lunch, we said adieu to all our guests. We paid the restaurant 1,500 pesos all up including lunch, cake, drinks and white doves. We went home. We opened the presents. By this time, Roger, our photographer cousin, would have gone the other way, so there were no photos of the opening of presents. We received a few items including an arinola (portable metal urinal) for good luck. And to our delight, we received 3,000 pesos in cash, enough to cover the reception costs. And enough to give us a start at life with a surplus.

We then went for a siesta. And everything was normal as if it was just another day. We possibly watched PBA game that night where Toyota and Crispa were versing each other. The next day, we went to the gym.

There was no honeymoon. In a couple of days, I had to leave my new husband and went to an out-of-town national conference for a few days. In a few more days, my cousin Roger has developed the pictures and sent me the hard copies together with the film. I reprinted a few copies of some choice shots and sent to it to our guests as a thank you card.

I also went to National Bookstore to buy a reasonably value-for-money wedding photo album and arranged the photos in chronological order. Upon completion, this wedding album was never to be seen again.

30 years on, my darling husband takes interest in our wedding album. Today has brought back memories of the day. From our humble beginnings to where we are now, I can say that like a tree we have grown. All our hard work has now paid off. The fruits are ripe for the taking.

30 years does not seem long. We still enjoy our afternoon siestas. We still enjoy watching NBA games. We still go to the gym together. Life is still simple, and we are still who we are.

Upon reflection many things have happened in 30 years. It's a good number to reflect on one's relationship to see what one has achieved and what one wants to look forward to. In 30 years, we raised 2 fine young men that we are proud of; we have weathered many storms and rose up to our challenges; we have built a happy home sweet home; we have visited a few beautiful cities around the world; we continued to work as a team, work towards our goals and always aimed for our surplus; we always help and support each other to become better versions of ourselves; we continued to love and respect one another; we continued to pray for God's grace.

My simple wedding album which has been stored for a few decades created my quiet reflection for today that I am no longer anxious of poverty. After 30 years, we are no longer poor. We are rich because of age and experience. We are rich in friends and rich in happiness. We are rich in love. We are rich in God's grace.

30 years on, we are still $E=MC^2$. My engineer, you are my energy, my light and my massive love of my life. Thank you for 30 years of blissful wedded life. Happiness and love everlasting.

To our family and friends who have continued to help and support us over the years, we say thank you. You are our foundation of strength. Thank you for the special greetings over the past few days. We are truly grateful for such show of love and affection.

31 December 2016

2016 Year in Review

Saying thank you and goodbye to fabulous 2016. HAPPY NEW YEAR!!

It's that time of the year again to reflect on our 365 days trip around the sun. And be grateful.

In January, we began by celebrating Aunty Sally and Uncle Roger's 50th Wedding anniversary. My mum and fav sister Aldrina travelled from California to join us. Major milestones such as this are truly precious gems and family reunions are the best part of this gathering. This must be one of the highlights of 2016.

The celebrations continued when Lolo Nap turned 80 years old in the same month. More milestones followed as we helped celebrate the birthdays of our very special family and friends. Hayden turned 7, Alex turned sweet 16, Jessica turned 21, Tristan turned 40, Pinky turned 50, Roger also turned 50, Eric turned 55, Susan turned 60, Uncle Roger turned 75. And Lolo Ben would have turned 85. To remember Lolo Ben, we had the Carols in the Valley on his natal day. All birthdays were celebrated in their own special way with Roger's Hawaii 5-0 swim party as one of my favourites. Of course, all other birthdays were celebrated too. Eric's theme was a Mahjong ParTea. Craig and Cora's combined birthday was a Triple MMM (Midyear Mahjong Madness). Egon's birthday was Mahjong Thai-O when he specifically wanted Thai Viet food. Ahhhh, that mahjong fever has really got Team Dural hot! Mahjong Thai-O (In cases you didn't get that, in Tagalog, Mahjong tayo – Let's play Mahjong)! Oh please!

And so….. Mahjong became the usual order of our weekends – our recent discovery for family bonding, which in my childhood days were totally disallowed by my parents. Because of its gambling element, it's automatically evil – from their point of view! If only my mum knew….. OMG, I will truly be in trouble!

But I don't know what the magic of mahjong brings. There is a certain unexplained spell, a cross between enchanting and captivating, that's quite fun, addictive and quite relaxing. Besides, I just do it because there has been some news article that links mahjong and the prevention of Alzheimer's disease. So…. Mag Mahjong Thai-O!

We got some breaks from swimming on the table. We indulged in a few entertainments. We watched The Illusionist 1903 at the Sydney Opera House in January with Lola Pary, Lolo Nap, Levi, Paulette, Violy, Egon, Eric and Cora. We watched a couple of live shows at the Riverside Theatre including The Doris Day story…. Motown Music and Whitney Houston. We enjoyed Ghost The Musical at the Theatre Royal in May. At the State Theatre, we "almost" enjoyed Georgie Girl, The Musical. Thank you to a horrifying experience of a pensioner whose bowel movements became uncontrollable. Say no more. We enjoyed a soul/funk night with Bump city at the Camelot lounge. We watched Singing in the Rain at The Lyric Theatre at The Star in August to celebrate my birthday. Eric enjoyed the Blue Man at Solaire Theatre in September. Thank you to the Catabijans for a very generous treat. In November, we thoroughly enjoyed a Filipino concert - Ogie Alcacid at Rooty Hills RSL with Laurence, Grace, TP and Mary Ann. Egon and Uncle Levi attended the Cold Play concert in December. Wow! That's entertaining!

We had a few overseas visitors during the year. Mum and fav sister Aldrina visited in January where we enjoyed knocking on and entering to as many doors of Mercy as we can. 2016 was designated as an extraordinary jubilee year of mercy by Pope Francis. This was one my most blessed moments especially shared with mum and sis. Cousin Gel came in March for her working holiday. Danny and Joe Tuason visited us in August. We enjoyed a full day in the Blue Mountains and another day in the city of Sydney capturing the blue hour of The Harbor Bridge and the Sydney Opera house. Cousin Vic and Belen Pascual also visited us in October. We had a great family reunion meeting Mabelle and Justin. Adriana from Colombia was also one of our special guests during the year. Ritchie, Eric's one and only brother-in-law, came in November to spend awesome quality time with lovely wife Paulette. As I am writing this journal, Miguel and his girlfriend Ceara from San Francisco are here as our last visitors for the year.

I had some girly days and nights out with my lovely lovely friends and family to catchup on the goss. A day out at Barangaroo with Alma. Couple of lunches and dinner with Marie and Gerlie. Another couple of brunch and dinner with Marichu, Dina, Pinky, Tonette, Dess, Yoly, Ellen and Luchie. My favourite part was our girly weekend away with Aunt Sally and cousins Rosallie and Regina when we braved the storms to Port Stephens and ended up inside the hotel room talking and laughing and talking and laughing and more talking and more laughing. So so fun to be with all these remarkable women in my life.

Eric and myself had a mini break during Easter. We spent a few days in Kiama where we enjoyed the sun, sea, sand, pristine forest, natural and green surrounds, lots of fresh air and a relaxing massage. The long trek to the waterfalls was the highlight of this trip.

In April, we witnessed Theresa and Ian's fabulous wedding at the Deckhouse. Lovely lovely Izzy's speech was so heartwarming and totally unforgettable. That was definitely one for the books.

The highlight of our year would be sister **Liz** and Jay-Ar Simangan's wedding in September where all the elements of happiness and love were in one space and time. Weddings are always beautiful. But this one was extraordinary! The bride was exquisitely stunning. The groom was equally gorgeous. The whole entourage was extremely charming. Baby Carlisle was cute as a button. The day was glorious. Even the traffic in Manila was quite tamed. Everything was perfect! Without enough notice, I was asked to do a wedding speech, which left me terrified to the max. When delivering my speech, there was no dry eye in the room. I wasn't sure if the guests felt sorry for me trembling throughout the speech or possibly, just possibly, I may have struck a chord and touched their hearts. Sorry guys I made you cry.

The best part of the wedding, well one of the best, is that the video of the wedding day was shown at the end of the wedding! We've attended many weddings in our lifetime, but we've never attended one which has shown the video right on the day of the wedding! Absolutely remarkable! Technology has definitely stepped up.

This wedding was the main reason we travelled to the Philippines. But before and after the wedding, we took the opportunity to visit the marvelous tourist cities of the Philippines and spend some quality time with family. It was a great family reunion with Eder and Blue from Texas, sis Aldrina from California and our local gracious hosts my brother Kuya Bet Laverenti and Grace .

Eric also had an opportunity to attend a family reunion with the Narcisos who are hosting 2017 Grand family Reunion. It was not a planned event but the stars aligned that day, cousins from overseas were also visiting Manila - Caloy and Sara, Kuya Mike and Ate Agnes.

We toured a few cities/provinces: Bohol, Quezon, Vigan, Paoay, Burgos, Pagudpud, Batac, La Union, Manaoag, Legazpi, Sorsogon.

We experienced new thrills: Riding an ATV, Bike ziplining, sand dune-ing in a 4x4, Snorkling in a fish sanctuary, learning pottery, patting a python, eating pinakbet pizza, chilli ice cream, malunggay ice cream, kare kare pasta, the list goes on and on.

The day after the wedding, like a group honeymoon, we visited dad's tombstone in Lopez, Quezon. As a family, we prayed and sang and kept vigil. We spent the afternoon introducing Jay-Ar to the rest of the Zamora clan.

Our 2016 is like Liz's wedding – there's something old, something new, something borrowed and something blue.

Our something old would be looking after our health. Spiritual health comes first. So our Sunday mass attendance is on top of the list. We continued to Thank and Praise God the Almighty, from whom all things come. To look after our physical aging bodies, we continued to enjoy our daily exercises. Eric would wake up at 5 am to hit the gym at opening time of 5:30am. I continued to attend my Wednesday yoga. Our Fridays continued to be our swim days at the local pool.

My something new is not one. There's a few of them. "They" were quite exciting. In January, I managed to finally get rid of all my curtains. We installed plantation shutters because I was getting sick from all the dirt and dust of curtain fabric. We also finally got the chance to install new air conditioning system at home, something more efficient and economical. We got rid of our 20-year old leather lounge and replaced it with a new one. Craig finally got his first new car (except it's not really new because it's a demo stock). I finally had new lawns. We managed a mini garden make over, replaced our lawns with Sir Walter Buffalo lawns (whatever it means) after 16 years in Barangay Dural. And…..and….and, as if I wasn't busy enough, I managed to squeeze in our bathroom renovations (3 upstairs and 1 downstairs) towards the end of the year! Whew!

My something blue was losing my friend Linda with her battle with cancer. Rest in peace lovely Linda. I miss you dearly. Her demise reminds me of my something borrowed which is our life. One day, any day, last day…. It came for her.

At work, I saw 80 new clients during the year. Each of them had their own story to tell, stories of struggles and pain and hopelessness. Stories of men and women stuck in circumstances, some within their own control and yet some, outside of their control. My work involves supporting individuals who are stuck. Stuck at life. My work is to help them get unstuck so they can move forward and have a more enriching and happier life experience.

I sit here and share my 365 days trip around the sun. From my own lens, I share my view of my wonderful 2016. My 2016 was not 365 everyday wonderful. There were good days and not so good days. There were days when there were challenges to take, issues to manage, conflicts to resolve and hard decisions to make. This is our something borrowed. This is every human being's life. We're all humans and like each of my clients, we each have a story to tell.

It has been a very very busy year. I am tired. I am happy tired. I am a bit sick as write this down. I have been coughing relentlessly over the past few weeks. As I write and as I cough, I wonder how between doing my laundry and ironing and cleaning the kitchen and grocery shopping and all other things, how I was able to pack these "something borrowed" all in. I'm happy for my 2016 story.

Today marks our 32nd wedding anniversary. This is not only MY 2016 story. It is OUR 2016 story.

With our "something borrowed cut" short with each 365- day merry-go-round the sun, our lens are focused on productive thoughts, behaviour and enriching experiences to view OUR life story. Life is short. View it well. Live it well.

Happy anniversary to my wonderful, wonderful husband, life travel companion, best friend, amazingly awesome love of my life.

Thank you 2016 for a most magnificent and fabulous adventure!!

HAPPY NEW YEAR TO ALL!!!

HAPPY EVERYTHING!!!!

August 2017

We are blessed (100 Years Anniversary of Fatima Apparition)
Home Sweet Home.

I'm finally home in Sydney after a lengthy trip to accompany my mum to her pilgrimage throughout Portugal, Spain and France. My wonderful sister Aldrina Zamora also joined the trip. I travelled to San Francisco from Sydney to join the rest of the 41 pilgrims from The Our Lady of Perpetual Help Parish in Daly City.

I shared a bit of our experiences through the photo albums I've created in FB as we visited the holy sites. It was unimaginable for my 84-year old mum that she has been able to travel to these beautiful and blessed places. She kept on saying "We are blessed, we are so blessed." She must have repeated this over a thousand times, maybe two thousand.... over and over again. Throughout the cities of Frankfurt, Lisbon, Fatima, Avila, Madrid, Zaragoza, Lourdes, Barcelona, Montserrat and Munich, my sister has patiently pushed her wheelchair with a little help from me.

We enjoyed the Centennial celebration of the apparition of the Mama Mary in Fatima. We visited the homes of the children in Aljustrel and Valinhos where Mama Mary and the angel appeared to them several times. We joined holy processions in Fatima and in Lourdes. We joined in the celebration of the holy Eucharist every single day in glorious chapels, magnificent churches, grand basilicas in all the cities that we visited. We prayed the holy rosary in different languages. We visited majestic places of natural beauty between Spain and France. We revisited history. We toured world class modern cities. We learned a lot. The list is endless. But most of all, we enjoyed our time spent together with mum..... in the hope that she remembers it.

We returned to San Francisco on Saturday, July 29 and I spent a few extra days with mum, sis and her family.

Courtesy of my college friend Minda, I had one day (reprieve from daughter duties) to enjoy San Francisco surrounds. Minda and her lovely family took me to the Palace of Fine Arts, Fort Baker Fishing Pier, Muir Woods and we enjoyed lunch at The Russian River Brewery in Sta. Rosa.

The next few days were spent with more bonding with mum and sis. We had a relaxing day at the Kenwood Inn and Spa in the enchanting Sonoma County. According to mum, this was her best day when 2 daughters (of 6 siblings) and 3 grandchildren (of 16) were all around her to shower her with love and attention. We were listening to the stories of her childhood, stories of her mum, dad and siblings, stories of her first grade teacher . We joined her dip in our private hot spa as we shared the Sonoma wine, meat, cheese and cracker charcuterie board throughout the day. We ended with a Thai dinner in Petaluma in E-Saan Thai.

The next day, we spent time in mum's happy place in the Jewish Community Centre (JCC) in San Rafael where I joined her in her aqua aerobics class. Mum enjoyed her water exercise with me and introduced me to her teacher and her senior friends. I can see the sparkle in her eyes as she splashed the water and do the routines. She was so cute and quite proud that she is still able to enjoy this. This is truly her happy place.

I also joined swim coach sis in a few swim laps in the outside pool in JCC on a perfect hot summer day. We ended the day with dinner at Sol Food with the grandchildren and 1 great grandchild, Benjamin, his name taken from Lolo Ben. Uncle Lito Sion also joined us. Mum was so pleased to see grandchild Randall and great grandchild Benjamin who she has not seen for around 6 years. She wondered if Benjamin will ever know and recognise her. Randall spent a few more moments with mum when we had ice cream at Terra Linda. Mum spoke of the days when she used to look after Randall and Franky in their younger days when dad and mum lived in Las Gallinas.

After weeks of traveling overseas and days of unusual treats, Mum was very tired and asked that we take her back to her senior home. It was my sister's first respite from care after 3 weeks.

While mum took a rest (which was also our rest), my ever generous sis treated me to a simmer down day at the Imperial Spa in San Francisco where every inch of our body was cleansed by a Korean body scrub and bathed in warm milk like princesses of ancient past. A total knock down experience for sis and myself after days of caring for mum! It was an absolutely divine experience. After which, we quickly walked around the Bay city. We enjoyed our lunch of clam chowder sour dough bread, turkey sandwich and Asian chicken salad in Boudin Breads. I'd say that this was sisterhood at its best!

A few hours later, we picked up mum to attend the first Wednesday Novena mass at Our Lady of Perpetual Help church in Daly city. I was surprised that my lovely sis organised a mass intention for my birthday and the parish priest blessed me. Again, mum muttered "We are blessed. We are so blessed." We met Jenny, Ate Rosalina and Ate Ethel (pilgrims from our group) at church and we said hi to them and a few chit chats. Mum asked who these people were. She asked us why we knew them. We reminded her that they were part of our pilgrim family and they cared for her while we were on tour. Mum does not remember any of these.

Mum asked that we have dinner after mass. We stopped by Goldilock's which was close to church and sis kindly got me a

Mangolicious birthday cake. And mum was excited for the birthday cake just like a child.

Meanwhile I received a heart warming thoughtful birthday song from my dear loving husband via FB. Overwhelmed with joy and happiness, I showed mum and she said, "We are blessed. We are so blessed."

The next day was the day of my flight back to Sydney. My friend, Del of 35 years, visited mum and brought some yummy turon for mum. Mum doesn't recognise Del anymore. And she said to her "Pardon me that I don't recognise you. Sometimes, I don't recognise my kids too."

After Del and I returned from lunch, we quickly organised my luggage to head off to San Bruno for my farewell dinner and birthday celebration at Cabalen. We were joined by my friend Malou and her husband Odie, mum, sis, 4 grandchildren and little Benjamin and his friend. We had dinner, cake and off to the airport we went.

Saying farewells at airports is my most dreaded part. This time, it's more difficult. My mum's signs of dementia have become more evident. As we said our good byes, I can't help but cry. Mum only remembers that "We are blessed. We are so blessed." But she remembers very little of our recent pilgrimage trip and the recent days we spent together. She asked me about Barcelona or Fatima or Madrid or Montserrat. And she asked if she has been there with me and what it was like to be there. She asked me to remind her what the place was like and what we did and what we saw. I showed her photos and she said, she didn't know that she travelled to those places. She told me at the airport that she wished I stayed a bit longer so she could have taken me to JCC so we could have a swim together so she can introduce me to her swim teacher and friends. She said she wished she was able to take me to her senior home and show me where she lives. I cried because she has forgotten that we have actually done this in the last 4 days. And I cried some more because I don't know when is the next time I will see her. And in that next time if she will still recognise me. A few times in Spain and France, she asked me who I was, it flashbacked on me at the airport, that one day in the future, she will no longer recognise me. I cried because in my rush to get to the boarding gate, I forgot to tell her that even if she forgets everything, I want her to remember that I love her or that somebody loves her.

As I celebrate my birthday enroute to Sydney, I quickly checked my FB at the gates before boarding. I have notifications of friends and family sending PMs on my messenger, writing birthday wishes on my wall, creatively posting pretty pictures/ collages, gorgeous messages, liking/reacting to other posts and leaving delightful lovely heart warming comments on my wonderful husband's love song. I thought I had time before boarding to thank everyone for their thoughtful greeting and well wishes. But we were called to board immediately.

After 14 hours of air time, I am in Sydney. I am finally home. 2 days have lapsed (crossing the international dateline) since my highly emotionally charged birthday and still haven't thanked everyone. I am writing in the middle of the night coping with jetlag and experiencing some form of separation anxiety from mum and sis.

For all of you who have kindly remembered me on my birthday, I sincerely thank you, for taking time out from your busy schedules to greet me. Thank you for the friendship we share.

Thank you to my most gorgeous sister, Aldrina, who has been there and has co-created so much unforgettable moments to cherish. I wish to thank my most wonderful husband who has made this trip possible as a birthday present to me, my mum and sis. Thank you for your alluring birthday love song that has made me feel at home away from home. Thank you for everything and all the support you gave me throughout this trip and your loving welcome home.

I honour my mum on my natal day. She deserves the well wishes, the love songs, the beautiful tapestry of kind words, pretty pictures, amazing thoughts written on my timeline. Birthdays remind me of time.... Time for more human experiences.... Time to think and feel and see and savour each living breathing moment..... Time to be with those we love and enjoy the things we enjoy doing. Time to remember our blessings..... even if dementia has taken them away....even if all memories have gone.

As my mum remembers, "We are blessed. We are so blessed."

January 2023

Crazy Rich Asian with high school friends

An out of town trip to Calatagan, Batangas to kick off LSQC 78 45th high school reunion.

It's more of a scene in Crazy Rich Asian movie, as we are invited to this lush 3 hectare beach front property south of Manila. The property is a rest house of one of LSQC 78 graduates, complete with well manicured gardens and fountains, walkways, go carts, golf buggy, swimming pool, whirlpool spa, private beach with jetski and boats, a helipad, resort style accommodation of many rooms, butlers, chef, white uniformed house staff, masseurs, you name it!

What a privilege to be invited. We were treated to cocktails by the beach as we watched the fantastic sunset of Hawaiian theme night, enjoying the company of friends, complete with live band music and fantastic entertainment. Your choice of drink - red wine, brandy, beer, fizzy drinks, bubbly, whatever your heart desires!!

The spa was heated to perfection; the clear water of the pool was so inviting.

At dinner time, crispy skin lechon was served together with a combination of Italian fare pasta, seafood chowder, bolognaise.... and traditional Filipino flavours of grilled bangus, vegetarian lumpia, shanghai, chicken curry and fresh ripe mangoes.

Wow!!! What an absolute treat. But that's just the tip of the iceberg. More more fun followed, as each of us enjoyed each other's company reminiscing high school days, lots of light banter, corny dad jokes, laughter, fun and 45 years of friendship.

The night never ends. But the body must rest. The life of seniors celebrated here at this magical place. Totally enchanting!!!!

Thank you so much for this amazing experience!!! We are so grateful to be part of this blessed circle.

31 December 2024

40th Wedding Anniversary

Thank you 2024 Welcome 2025

What a fitting end to 2024, to celebrate our 40th wedding anniversary with our nearest and dearest with a big bang.

Thank you to all of you who sent your wonderful messages of love and support and to those who have joined us in our joyful celebration and renewal of vows.

2024 was incredibly rich in human experiences. We had 3 weddings, 3 christenings and attended 5 funerals of 11 deaths in the family.

We enjoyed 6 holidays with family and friends. We visited 33 new cities in the 7 countries we travelled to.

We celebrated 17 major birthdays and anniversaries of family and friends including Ate Violy's 80th and Captain Roy's 60th. We entertained 4 visiting guests from overseas and played tourist guide with them.

We saw 17 musicals/shows between Manila, Europe and Australia.

- Pingkian at the Cultural Center of the Philippines
- Musical Romance in Vienna at Palais Eschenbach
- Death of a Salesman at Theatre Royal
- Burt Bacharach at The Sydney Coliseum
- Six The Musical at The Theatre Royale
- Dear Evan Hansen at The Roslyn Packer Theatre
- Jesus Christ Superstar at The Capitol Theatre

- Desperado Night of Music
- World of Musicals
- Gaslight at The Riverside Parramatta theatre
- And Juliet at The Lyric theatre
- Billy Joel Show
- Sunset Blvd at The Sydney Opera House
- Guitarra at The Chatswood COncourse
- Sister Act at The Capitol Theatre
- Catch me if you can at The Blue Mountains Theatre
- M7 Merrylands RSL

We watched thousands of episodes between Dirty Linen, Linlang, Lavender Fields, Maria Clara, Pulang Araw, Black Rider, Widow's war, Outlander, What's Next, American Idol, Australian Idol, and of course, our favourites Batang Quiapo and Jeopardy.

We endlessly laughed at episodes of Virtuous Business and Fiery Priest and marvelled at Squid Games 2.

Visiting Ephesus, Turkey sparked our interest in ancient history and led us to spend hours watching Troy; Alexander the making of a God; Roman empire; Ancient Rome – The rise and fall of an empire, The destiny of Rome.

This Olympic year, we watched all Olympic events possible. After that (and maybe even before the games), Eric was glued to the TV trying to watch all of the basketball games available including NBA, NCAA, NBL, Asian basketball, UAAP. And what a historic gold medal win for the Cardinal and Golds!

We had several lovely catch ups with our favourite friends over dinner, lunch, park walks, picnics, food tour, girls sleep over, yoga fund raiser, trivia night, first Friday masses and church events such as San Lorenzo Ruiz and Father Fernando's (our parish priest) 25th anniversary ordination.

We tried to stay fit and healthy in body and mind. I continued my free Duolingo lessons in Spanish to help sharpen my brain.

But 2024 saw our declining state of health as we age. Our bathroom now has a shower stool for seniors to keep safe during bath time. Eric started to wear hearing devices and on some days needs a walking stick to help him.

I have sadly cancelled my 28-year gym membership due to my vertigo attacks, that is not helping in my yoga class. My ailing knees, back and shoulders due to osteo arthritis have progressively continued to cause discomfort and pain.

This year, we started having regular appointments with the GP and some specialists – Cardiologist, Ortho, ENT. We are expecting surgeries in 2025.

Even our house hold appliances have started to break down. To catch up with technology, the old solar panels were replaced by a more efficient and updated model. The garden fences were partially replaced due to wear and tear. Our refrigerator broke down on Christmas morning (of all days!).

Our 2024 behaved so much like the share market, with its unpredictable highs and lows.

My absolute low was the loss of our dear Mommy Cons that left us grieving for a long time, maybe until now. This was followed by the shocking loss of our dear friend Yoly, who passed away straight after our River cruise holiday in Europe. Even more heart breaking was the loss of Aunty Luz and which was followed by her loving husband Uncle Pete in a matter of weeks.

Another low, was being on holiday during a strong typhoon Carina. No matter what great plans you make, the good weather is something you can only hope for.

Our 2024 was not all low. It was actually a fantastic year to keep in the memory banks. Like long term investments with peaks and troughs, these precious memories will increase in value in later years.

There were so many firsts for us. Our first river cruise with friends when we embarked on group tour from Amsterdam to Budapest (covering Netherlands, Germany, Austria, Czech Republic, Hungary); our first time to release endangered turtles into wildlife in Bataan; our first hotel cave accommodation in Cappadocia, Turkey; our first in-flight illness and ambulance waiting for us at the tarmac between airports; our first Metro ride to Barangaroo on opening week.

There were also so many items on my bucket list ticked — my dream to enter the Habsburg's Schonbrunn palace; my desire to visit Amsterdam; my curiosity to see Hagia Sofia and the Grand Bazaar in Istanbul; my wish to be between Asia and Europe in Bosphorus strait; my need to experience a Turkish hammam; my excitement to watch Australian Open live with friends; my hope to experience Galipoli on ANZAC day.... The list goes on.

But really, my all time highs, would be spending precious time with my family and friends.

Celebrating our 40th wedding anniversary was an absolute blessing and a perfect time to reflect on our highs and lows of 2024.

Thank you to all our guests for sharing this special milestone with us especially our senior family members Aunty **Sally Angara** and Lola **Pary Cardenas** for gracing the occasion.

Special thanks to **Brian Lorenz II** (and his team DJ Errol) who hosted and brilliantly managed the event to everyone's delight.

Grateful to **Liezel Zamora Simangan Jay Simangan** and **Regina Angara** for doing all of the hard work and special details leading up towards the day.

Thank you to our angels and flower kids Kayleigh, Carl, Sophia and sometimes Stefan, for graciously providing that charming fun factor for each and every part of the program.

Thank you to **Roger Angara** for a wonderful speech with so much endearing, wise and kind words. Thank you to another Roger, Father **Roger Delmonte** , who despite his busy schedule, has taken time for us to bless and remind us of our love and commitment to each other, officiating our renewal of vows.

Grateful for all my friends and family who sent their messages of love.

Special thanks to Paulette **Card Paulette** for providing the party favours and to my good friend **Rex Betty Tanglao** for providing the most delicious cake we have ever tasted.

To our faithful friend **Augusto Roxas** , thank you for being our great photographer. To my best friend **Pinky Bautista** and Gerry, what will we do without your super fun photobooth? Thank you.

To my children **Craig Winston Cardenas** and **Egon Cardenas** for gathering together messages from overseas and organising this part of the program, our hearts go out in gratitude to both of you. Thank you for being our children, our pride and joy.

To my partner in crime **John Eric N Cardenas** for 40 years of love, thank you for being my loyal constant. 40 years have been swift and smooth. Like the share market, if we keep investing in the good that we already know and works for us, it can only go up and grow in the long term.

Our 40 years anniversary celebration was a year end thanksgiving event that we will all remember with fondness and fun. It will be my personal anchor in 2025 to keep me grounded and safe. We have been given a new name: Life Lovers.

We will follow that path to loving life large.

Cheers to good health, peace, great friendships and wonderful adventures in 2025!

31 December 2025

2025 Year End Journal

"For better for worse, for richer or for poorer, in sickness and in health, to love and to cherish..."

Today marks anniversary number 41 for us. As always, first and foremost, we are grateful.

We started 2025 with a hospital procedure, a cardiac ablation in January. In December, we ended with another hospital procedure, a simultaneous bilateral knee replacement surgery for Eric. From the heart to the knees, the message is clear – we're in the stage when life asks for the strength of the heart to keep beating and the humility of the knees to keep bending.

The heart is where courage and love lives, where dreams are born, where we hold the people and the moments that matter most. The knees remind us that we are never walking alone; they bend in prayer, in gratitude, in humility and surrender to ask for God's grace. We need our hearts and knees to keep going.

2025 was a year when we embraced the strength and the humility we needed to move forward and keep going in the years ahead.

Between these hospital gigs, we had an unbelievable year of grace, filled with so much life, love and adventures.

If you know us, we love our family bonds, our circle of good friends, our travel, our shows, our celebrations, our new learnings and our quiet down time. Each year, our year end journal lists most of them. This year is no different.

2025 saw us celebrating so many milestone birthdays – Gerlie's 60th, Craig's 40th, Aunty Sally's 85th, Alvin's 50th, Lola Pary's 90th, Hayden's 16th, Olivia's 18th, Tita Annies' 87th , Gus' 80th, Evelyn's 70th. We counted 35 events in our calendar including Alex and Matt's engagement party in February; Lola Pary's grand 90th birthday celebration in May; Pithu and Kothu night with our Sri Lankan friends in June; Tonette's double baby shower for her 2 grandbabies in July; 50th wedding anniversary of Ate Violy and Kuya Boy in August; Iris and Kevin's wedding reception in November;

We welcomed a few visitors in Sydney – cousin Henry, Marichu and classmate Carmela in April; cousin Stella and family in June; Iris in June.

We enjoyed our shows together with our Show friends, we now have a group called Show friends. We counted 18 shows: Beatle Magic in January (straight from the hospital after the cardiac ablation!); Carole King and James Taylor in February; Hadestown; MJ The Musical; Charlie and the Chocolate Factory; Footloose; Hank Marvin; Jersey Boys; Here you come again; Commodores; The book of Mormon, among many more. We enjoyed Back to The Future The Musical, so much, we watched it 2x!

We saw some Filipino shows and concerts: OPM South Border in September and Song of the Fireflies in November.

It's like we turned "watching" into our new career in senior living, we indulged in more watching at home. We continued to watch Filipino tv series – Batang Quiapo; Saving Grace; Pamilya Sagrado; Incognito; Sins of the Father; What lies beneath; Roja. We watched some Filo films: My Future You; Uninvited; Green Bones; Monday First Screening.

Of course, he continued to watch all things basketball and sports on tv!

We watched some food shows: Somebody Feed Phil; 1 in 7641; Eva Longoria: Searching for Mexico.

Korean tv series remained in our watchlists. We enjoyed Squid games 3; Model Family; Worst of Evil; Nine Puzzles; Bon Apetit your Majesty; Good Bad Mother; Unwritten Seoul ; Beyond the Bar; The Dream life of Mr. Kim.

What is it, that when watching food shows and Korean tv series, that awakens your senses all at once and tempts you to try these food? What magic is there behind the bowl of kimchi or chop sticks lifting japchae; group of family and friends slurping shared meals and side dishes? Beyond the food, I guess it's the culture of togetherness, the comfort of good relationships, and the rituals of life events.

So, after each episode, we tried to organise random lunch and dinner with family and friends. We counted 12 of these catchups throughout 2025 eating not only Korean food but trying different kinds of cuisine – Portuguese, Italian, Hainanese, Japanese, Cantonese, Korean and Filipino street food, of course. Needless to say, I have gained considerable amount of unwanted kilograms. Blame it on metabolism! (Not to mention sitting too long on the couch watching too much while munching much more!) Shame! Haha!

Ageing has started to show. This year, most weeks, we had doctor's appointments of different kinds.

I had an ENT appointment in the first quarter to treat my unusually frequent nose bleeds. In March, I experienced the most painful nasal polyp cauterisation, without anaesthetics. Not only was it extremely painful, it deformed the right side of my face from the many instruments inserted in my tiny little nostril, all at once. I counted at least 5 including a mirror, a cauterising instrument, 2 metal rods to create space for the mirror and the machine and another metal rod to hold cotton balls to absorb blood! Ouch!

I had a series of vestibular physio to treat my vertigo. I had a series of physio and visit to the acupuncturist to treat my lower back pains and upper back shoulder pains. I was diagnosed with DDD from L1 to L4 and S1 to S2.

Meanwhile, Eric continued his physio until the day he was ready for this bilateral knee surgery in December. He continued to see his cardiologists for constant monitoring of his heart strength.

But all these didn't stop us from ticking our bucket list and doing what retirees try to do more of. Travel.

This year was another 7 new countries visited and at least 24 new cities enjoyed. Absolutely one of the highlights of our year was finally travelling to 5 countries in South America (after so many times of cancellation) and 2 countries in Asia. Chile, Brazil, Argentina, Peru, Ecuador, Singapore and Malaysia.

It was an unbelievable trip climbing the heights of Macchu Picchu and walking the volcanic rocks of the Galapagos, in our health conditions. It was a miracle, we made it through!

This trip was the biggest trip we embarked as we went through 15 flights and 1 cruise, over a period of 6 weeks, ticking off my wish list including Rio de Janeiro, Christ the Redeemer, Sugarloaf mountain, Ipanema, Sacred Valley, Lake Titicaca, watching a Tango show in

Buenos Aires, experiencing the roar of the Iguazu falls at the Devil's throat, experiencing the Peruvian altitudes and the wonders of the Incan culture, Being at Latitude 0.00.00 in Quito, seeing the 100 year old tortoise in Galapagos, star gazing in the middle of the earth so close to the equator, watching the sunset in Hannga Roa, seeing the moias in Rapa Nui, and so much more. The number of cathedrals we visited during easter on this jubilee year made us feel like we were real pilgrims of hope, entering designated sacred doors. An absolute blessing!

The trip to Singapore – Malaysia was a short one. This was a food trip after watching the food shows, we needed to taste our list of food from chicken rice, hokkien mee, bak kuh the, salted egg prawns, sambal stingray, chilli crab, ondeh ondeh, rotiboy and so much more. Singapore was an amazing reunion with great friends and family.

Ageing makes us feel that our time is slowly running out. One day, any day, could be my last day here on this earth on this way. It has given me a sense of urgency to do the more important things with the people that matters most.

2025 has seen a decline in health for some of my loved ones, experiencing terminal illness and long term health issues. I continue to pray for 6 of them daily. This year, we lost Ken, our 12-year old grandnephew from denge fever, lost two cousins, two aunts, 1 grandma and my best friend TP. It was tough.

Yet, life goes on.

In November, we travelled to the Philippines to attend my nephew's wedding - Bien and Babylyn. This should be the highlight of our quarter end. First time in 19 years, my siblings, 3 from the USA, 1 from the Philippines, 2 from Australia, have finally spent time together. My brother's wedding speech was touching. He said that "This is all about family."

The wedding was perfect - the weather, the venue, the planning of every single detail from the clothes, the timing, the food and drinks, the program, the videos, the speeches, the dance numbers, the party favours, the fireworks ... it was impeccable. It was the best wedding we have attended. Yet, what stood out was still the same. It was the blessing of family togetherness. It was our moment of belonging.

After the wedding, my brother organised a double christening for his grandchildren. As a reunion of generations, we enjoyed more family time and great bonding. We all felt the blessings flowed.

2025 is indeed another year of abundant blessing.

We had many new things and new experiences in 2025.

January saw us buying a new EV because we had a problem with our old Pulsar. In March, Craig had a car accident which has written off his vehicle. We were forced to get another new vehicle, in a matter of 2 months.

In February, we were gifted with a Flouna voucher. It's a magnesium float and a sauna combined. What a relaxing new experience. Also in February, with my group of long time kumare girl friends Jenn and Violy, we did a full day Korean scrub. What an enjoyable new experience with long tme friends! In September, Jenn and myself went to a full day spa, massage, facial mani, pedi, girls day out.

I had a day out at the Australian museum with Alma to see the Wonders of Peru. A new year's resolution to do something new each birthday.

At Church, I had the stations of the cross with Dess from March to April. We attended the wonderful Food fiesta in May. We were invited to attend the Bishop Vincent's anniversary mass and we were blessed for our 40th wedding anniversary. I attended first Friday masses with my friends Myrthel and Estrelita. In December, Egon attended with me and we won 2 raffle prizes!

Something big and something new, on my birthday, I pre launched my book to commence my authoring journey. It is entitled Live Wealthy Retire Happy – Embracing human experiences to live a life of abundance.

Every year, Eric buys me flowers for our anniversary. Because he is unwell this time, it was my turn to buy him flowers on our 41st wedding anniversary. Another new way to love and to hold.

Every new thing, every new experience, every new blessing. We thank 2025.

We wish everyone a very happy new year. Welcome 2026 with strong hearts and bended knees. Much love.

About the Author

Cora Cardenas defines herself as an ordinary human being. She was born and raised in the Philippines by struggling parents who believed that education was their only way out of poverty. She studied in St Paul College of Manila, an exclusive private school for girls, despite her parents' financial hardships. They believed that this would be the foundation of strong character, good values, refined breeding and eventually a fulfilling life of meaning and purpose.

She gained a bachelor's degree in Business Administration from the Philippine Women's University through a college scholarship. Cora is a CPA and has a master's degree in business management and human behaviour from Macquarie Graduate School of Management. She has 25 years of corporate finance experience in the pharmaceutical manufacturing industry.

Her volunteer work with the SISTER2sister program prompted her to help vulnerable members of the community by inspiring young girls to dream big and live fulfilling lives. She heeded a call to do community service after she completed a diploma from the Centre for Community Welfare Training, majoring in financial counselling.

Cora is now 15 years into financial counselling, helping clients who are undergoing financial stress and hardship. She believes that money touches every aspect of human life. With her personal experiences with money, managing debt, creating wealth and building a happy retirement, she changes lives every day.

In her retirement years, she is dedicating two days a week at the community centre to do the work that she loves and, according to her own words, '**the work that heaven assigned for me**'.

She is happily married to her husband of 40 years. Eric and Cora migrated to Australia with their two young children in 1991. Similar to many migrants' stories, they have experienced a mix of excitement, challenge, struggle and great outcomes.

It is her ultimate desire to see fewer people experiencing poverty. Through education and financial literacy, it is her dream to witness ordinary individuals like her enjoy true financial independence.

Notes